BALLADS

OF

NEW JERSEY

IN THE

REVOLUTION

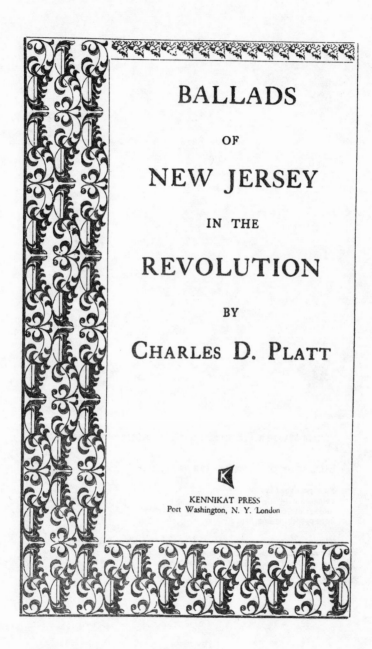

BALLADS

OF

NEW JERSEY

IN THE

REVOLUTION

BY

CHARLES D. PLATT

K

KENNIKAT PRESS
Port Washington, N. Y. London

MIDDLE ATLANTIC STATES HISTORICAL PUBLICATIONS SERIES NO. 9

BALLADS OF NEW JERSEY IN THE REVOLUTION

First published in 1896
Reissued in 1972 by Kennikat Press
Library of Congress Catalog Card No.: 76-186076
ISBN 0-8046-8609-2

The cooperation of Glassboro State College, Glassboro, New Jersey
in making the original copy of this book available from its
Stewart Collection is gratefully acknowledged.

IF I felt that these ballads were worthy of a formal dedication I should dedicate them to the two brothers whose labors in searching out and recording the traditions of Morris County in the Revolution awakened in my mind the desire to celebrate that history in verse.

These ballads are not a work of fiction. I have followed the historian closely, sometimes almost word for word. A list is given herewith of those historical works from which my information is derived.

These sources are referred to by number in the Table of Contents.

It will be seen that Books I., II., IV., and V., are chiefly based upon the Tuttle papers in Dawson's Magazine; while Book III. is chiefly taken from Mellick's Story of an Old Farm.

Messrs. Harper and Brothers have kindly permitted the use of some illustrations which appeared in connection with an article by Rev. Joseph F. Tuttle, D.D., in Harper's Magazine for February, 1859.

SOURCES.

✿✿✿✿✿✿✿✿✿✿✿

1. Bottle Hill, or Madison N. J., during the Revolution, by Rev. Samuel L. Tuttle. Dawson's Magazine.
2. Washington in Morris County, by Rev. Joseph F. Tuttle, D.D., Pres't of Wabash College, Indiana. Dawson's Mag.
3. The Story of an Old Farm, or Life in New Jersey in the Eighteenth Century, by Andrew D. Mellick, Jr.
4. Irving's Life of Washington.
5. Lossing's Field Book of the Revolution.
6. Bancroft's History of the United States.
7. Fiske's American Revolution.
8. Historical Collections of New Jersey.
9. County Histories of New Jersey.
10. Ashbel Green's Autobiography.
11. Topography of Washington's Camp of 1780, by Emory McClintock, LL.D.
12. Wicke's History of the Oranges.
13. Hatfield's History of Elizabeth Town.
14. Private information.
15. Hageman's Princeton and its Institutions,
16. Lee's Surprise of Paulus Hook, by Charles H. Winfield, Esq.
17. Hardyston Memorial (Sussex Co.) by Rev. A. A. Haines.
18. Caldwell and the Revolution ; A Centennial Address, by Rev. Everard Kempshall, D.D., of Elizabeth, N. J.

CONTENTS.

✿✿✿✿✿✿✿✿✿✿✿✿

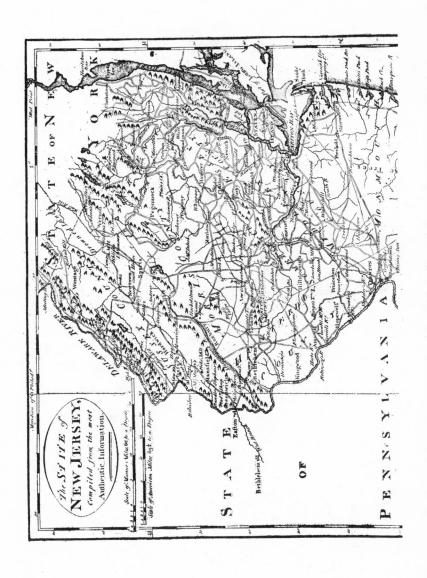

The State of
NEW JERSEY,
Compiled from the most
Authentic Information.

BOOK I

1776-1777

From LONG ISLAND to MORRISTOWN,

August 22, 1776—to January 6, 1777.

※❀❀❀❀❀❀❀❀❀❀❀❀

DISHEARTENED our forefathers were,
    Ay, sad of heart were they,
When at Long Island's luckless fight
    Our army lost the day.

And when that long retreat began,
    Till o'er the Delaware
Our leader fled, New Jersey's head
    Hung low in deep despair.

Through Newark and Elizabethtown
    He passed, and onward through
New Brunswick marched ; to Princeton next
    And Trenton ; full in view,

Upon their track the foe pursued
    And seized each place of strength,
Till o'er the Delaware our chief,
    Downhearted, crossed at length.

And then in prayer uplifted were
    The hearts of godly men
In many a Meeting House and home,
    That he might come again,

5

And drive the invaders from our land,
    Our cause and country save ;
That the Lord of hosts would guard our coasts
    And bless our patriots brave.

And come again he truly did
    That glorious Christmas night,
When at a stroke the spell he broke
    That o'er us cast its blight.

And when, just in the nick of time,
    The roads were frozen hard,
And our " old fox" was in a box,
    Cornwallis off his guard,—

Then like a flash he made a dash
    To Princeton town away,
Where George the Third—ill-omened word !—
    Quite " lost his head" that day.

Then, then we knew our leader true
    Was rightly in command ;
Our hopes grew strong that we ere long
    Should get the upper hand.

In spirits high our troops drew nigh
    To the hills of Morristown,
And there stayed they for many a day
    And gave those hills renown.

From Princeton on to Pluckamin
    By way of Rocky Hill ;
Through Basking Ridge, New Vernon, thence
    To Boisaubin's Gristmill;

6

By Moses Lindsley's corner then
  He marched along the road
That from Green Village leads unto
  The place where he abode.

'Twas in Loantaka they camped,
  Within that sheltering vale ;
And there they stay until the stings
  Of wintry rigor fail.

The LIFE in BOTTLE HILL and

MORRISTOWN.

THE troops were billeted where'er
  A roof could shelter give ;
Where once a quiet hamlet was
  Now thronging warriors live.

'Twas " Six men here !" " Twelve yonder !" and
  " Six officers must here
Their quarters make !" and welcome such,
  A safeguard from our fear.

7

The best rooms in the house were given
　　To these strange guests, the while
The family in the garret kept
　　Or dwelt in homely style

All in the kitchen ; there they slept
　　And there prepared their food ;
Scant were their comforts, but their hearts
　　Were schooled to fortitude.

The soldiers huddled in their rooms,
　　A stall served for a bed,
And there upon the floor at night
　　A couch of straw was spread.

There twelve and sometimes twenty lay,
　　All crowded in together,
Each in a single blanket wrapt
　　Through that stern winter weather.

Before great fires they laid them down
　　To dream of Freedom's rights,
And fought the cold as best they could
　　Through the bleak winter nights.

Our Washington his quarters made
　　At Freeman's Tavern then,
Just on the west side of the Green
　　In Morristown—'twas when

Brave Colonel Arnold kept the inn,
　　Of Sullivan's light horse,
And thither oft came men of might
　　Who officered our force.

8

There Generals Sullivan and Lee
 Have made their stay ; nay more,
" Old Put" was there and the debonair
 Young Hamilton, of yore.

In families throughout the town,
 Were quartered General Wayne
And General Maxwell,—well they served
 Their country's cause, those twain.

And here in pleasant social ways
 They lived the winter through,
And mingled with their cares some joys
 Befitting patriots true.

Three thousand in Loantaka
 Were camped in cabins rude,
Where hardship with relentless force
 Its sharp attacks renewed.

When, on the march from Trenton fight
 And Princeton, here they came,
The people all turned out to see
 And celebrate their fame.

The WINTER CAMP in LOANTAKA,
1777.

❈❈❈❈❈❈❈❈❈❈❈

LOANTAKA! Loantaka!
　　It is an Indian name;
The vale it took its name from the brook
　　That floweth through the same.

A stream it was, so limpid clear,
　　By gushing fountains fed,
With waters pure and welcome, sure,
　　To soldiers hard bestead.

'Twas wooded then, a lovely glen,
　　A valley fair to see;
All densely stood the unbroken wood,
　　From fence and dwelling free.

So here they camped when they had tramped
　　From Princeton all the way;
In seventy-seven, upon the sixth,
　　A January day.

They pitched their camp and through it made
　　A main street passing wide;
And in the midst a flagstaff set
　　For all the countryside.

And here on Grand Parade were seen
　　Our chiefs assembled all;
Both Wayne and Lee and Knox and Greene,
　　And their leader, staid and tall.

From miles around the people came,
    From miles around to see
The noble host that from our coast
    Should drive the enemy.

The CABINS in LOANTAKA.

NOW in the camp were cabins built
    For officers and men,
In blocks of three or four or five
    As best might fit the glen.

Three hundred cabins built they here,
    As often I've heard say,
Of logs rough-hewn, with clap-board roofs,
    They stood for many a day.

And doors and windows, too, they made
    With wooden hinge and latch ;
And mud for plaster served them well
    The gaping holes to patch.

Beyond the limits of the camp
    Were sentry houses made,
For faithful watch must still be kept
    'Gainst spy and midnight raid.

Within the lines no one might pass,
    But most of all by night,
Unless he showed a permit signed
    Or spoke that word of might,

The countersign, which opens wide
    The sacred doors that keep
The silent groups of patriot troops
    From peril while they sleep.

The PARSONS in the CAMP.

AND hither came good Parson Johnes,
    And Parson Green as well,
And Parson Caldwell, he who fought
    At Springfield, as they tell.

On Sabbath days he came to preach,
    If weather would allow,
From a stage set up on the Grand Parade—
    I fain would hear him now.

The sick and dying he would tend
    And speak the last sad word
When o'er some gallant comrade dead
    The burial rite was heard.

12

THE PARSONS IN THE CAMP.

A good and faithful man was he
    And feared not to be bold
If he might lead a precious soul
    Into the heavenly fold.

For in that rough, rude winter camp
    He came and went to save
The men who risked their life and all,
    Those warriors stern and brave.

And there was need, for on that camp
    There fell a fearful pest,
The small-pox, that malignant foe
    That works grim Death's behest.

It raged throughout the camp and slew
    Full many a soldier brave ;
Privates and officers alike
    It hurried to the grave.

Rude hospitals were made, and there
    The sick and dying lay ;
The church at Hanover was full
    Of patients in that day.

The dead were carried to their rest
    From hard-fought battle-fields ;
Now may their souls obtain at last
    The peace heaven's mercy yields.

13

The LOOKOUT at SHORT HILLS.

WHILE here the army camped, they set
 A sentinel band to stay
Above Short Hills and there keep watch
 As far as New York Bay.

To New York Bay they looked, and where
 The Island rises blue ;
Over Newark and Elizabethtown
 And Springfield was their view.

And toward the west, behind them lay
 · The hills of Morristown,
With a view due west to Basking Ridge
 And southward, looking down

On Middlebrook ; then to the north
 O'er Whippany and Montville ;
Away to Pompton—further where
 The Orange Mountains fill

The horizon—all this view was theirs
 From that fair look-out crown,
Upon the fields and vales and woods
 And rivers looking down.

And here how often Washington
 Stood gazing far away
And swept the field for signs of cheer
 To find instead dismay.

For, once, as here the General's look
    Was fixed, he gazing down
Beheld a sight he ill could brook,
    The fleet of the British crown.

And not long after came the raid
    Of Knyphausen and his men ;
But thanks to Watts and Caldwell's aid
    In haste they fled again.

Upon this height with outlook wide
    There was a cannon set;
An eighteen-pounder, and it boomed,
    As from a minaret

The Moslem calls to prayer ; so here
    Each half-hour, day by day,
On dark and stormy nights as well,
    This cannon boomed away

Whene'er the foe was seen astir,
    And it roused our minute-men ;
At times a beacon light was fired—
    Far flamed the tidings then.

Long did the memory of those days—
    The dismal booming gun,
The beacon spires of flaming fires,
    The quick, impatient run,

The cry, " to arms ! to arms !" and all
    The excitement of the hour—
Long did it linger in the hearts
    Of those who had felt its power.

TIDINGS OF

BURGOYNE'S SURRENDER.

✿✿✿✿✿✿✿✿✿✿✿

YET in those days were men who fled
And left the camp behind
To seek their homes, and oft, perchance,
For battle disinclined.

And some were hanged by martial law,
Some ran the gauntlet, scourged
By cruel blows that o'er the course
Their flagging footsteps urged.

Now when the army here had camped
Five months, as it may be,
They turned and went as they had come
To fight for liberty.

Then was Loantaka once more
A scene of gentle peace,
The peace that cometh in at door
When War's rude clamors cease.

So quiet filled this lovely vale
Until the tidings came
That made each heart with joy upstart
And put such peace to shame.

Oh glorious news! who could refuse
To join the glad huzzah!
For Gates has won! Burgoyne's undone!
Huzzah! Huzzah! Huzzah!

BURGOYNE'S SURRENDER.

From house to house the tidings flew,
    Loud rang the joyful cheers;
Each doubting heart now took a part
    And put away its fears.

'Twas in October of seventy-seven,
    A long-remembered day,
The seventeenth of the month, I ween,
    When the clouds were rolled away.

With illuminations and grand ovations
    And the flag on the liberty pole,
While guns were fired by men inspired—
    Our joy knew no control.

And well we might greet with delight
    The news of victory,
For none in all the land, I trow,
    Had suffered more than we.

We bore our share nor did we spare
    Our prayers nor strong right arm
To win the day that shall for aye
    Fill tyrants with alarm.

INCIDENTS OF 1776-77

JOHN WITHERSPOON.

PHILADELPHIA, JULY 4, 1776.

JOHN WITHERSPOON !—'tis a quaint old name,
But there it stands on the roll of fame
Among the foremost of our state
For power in counsel and debate.
A parson was he from over the sea,
A Scotch divine who was called to be
The head of the school that proudly bears
The name of our state—just climb the stairs
By which we mount from the railroad track
And soon we shall find what takes us back
To the olden time, a place that they call
By that quaint old name—'tis Witherspoon Hall.

But what of him ? Much more, in sooth,
Than I can tell; for not over youth
Alone did he rule, but men, as well,
Were swayed by the old man's power and spell.

An instance? Yes. 'Twas the fourth of July
In '76 and the hour was nigh
When the fate of a nation should hang in the scale—
This is no medieval tale
Of Sir Galahad and the Holy Grail,
But matter-of-fact, and a Jerseyman
The hero—find a better who can!

'Tis the fourth of July, a day, it appears,
When Congress meets; grave doubts and fears
Oppress their hearts, till the very air
Is a-quiver with struggling hope and despair.
Intent they listen to one who reads
A Declaration wherein he pleads
For the rights of man, bids patriots draw
The sword to uphold God's equal law.
For Independence he pleads, and all
Are thrilled with hope, yet feel the pall
Of possible failure that overhangs
The moment—a moment of bitter pangs,
When the birth-hour darkens the soul with pain,
Ere the life breaks forth that so long has lain
In hiding.   Such was the fateful hour,
A time when the secret springs of power
Are revealed, and the beat of each true heart
Is felt thro' the nation of which it is part—
When suddenly, mid the hush of fate,
Up rose John Witherspoon of our state.
His stalwart form full well they know
With its hoary crown as white as snow.
Firm was the old man's countenance

19

And keen the glint of his piercing glance
As he broke the silence of that room
With voice that had in it the stroke of doom.

" There is a time in the tide," quoth he,
" A nick of time, when the destiny
Of men and nations is fixed for aye,
And at such a time are we met to-day.
You all have heard—there is no need
That our country's cause should longer plead ;
One thing remains, let every man
Set his name to the deed, be it boon or ban.
For he who will not respond to the call
Of Freedom's voice, let him die a thrall !
These gray hairs of mine must soon descend
Into the sepulchre ; but my end
Shall come at the hands of the hangman ere
I swerve from my course as Freedom's heir."

The old man ceased and a deep-drawn sigh
Weut up from his hearers—the smothered cry
Of a new-born nation grew loud and clear,
Resolve was fixed—banished was fear.

And now you have heard how John Witherspoon broke
That fateful silence, and how he spoke,
And how it was that grave men as well
As youth came under his power and spell.

General CHARLES LEE at Basking Ridge, December 12, 1776.

❈❈❈❈❈❈❈❈❈❈❈

PART I.

O GENERAL LEE has come to town,
    A warrior bold is he;
Of all the generals in the land
    None may so valiant be;
Not General Gates, although he stands
    Well in the public eye,
Nor do the people in their hearts
    Set Washington so high.

For General Lee is a soldier bred,
    A warrior famed afar;
From Poland and Spain to Fort Duquesne
    He has studied the art of war.
In prompt despatch he has not his match,
    Nor will he hesitate;
A hero, in short, and has paid his court
    To Frederick the Great.

From Morristown he now has come.
    Upon his southward way,
To save the Jerseys from the foe
    In this our darkest day;
For Washington has made retreat
    Across the Delaware
And left the Jerseys to their fate,
    We're now in deep despair.

21

The British roam unhindered through
    The country, far and wide ;
They take our cattle and our sheep,
    Do what they will beside.
Oh would that this tedious fight would end
    Or never had begun ;
And yet, led on by General Lee,
    I trow 'twill soon be done.

PART II.

MAJOR WILKINSON RIDES FROM SUSSEX CO. TO MORRIS CO.

A horseman rides o'er the Jersey hills
    To seek for Washington ;
From the camp of Gates with a letter he comes,
    'Tis Major Wilkinson.
" O where is our gallant chief," quoth he,
    " The chief of our forces all ?
Who takes our part with a dauntless heart,
    Whatever may befall."

" O he hath crossed to the other side
    Of the river Delaware,
And ride you may for many a day
    Ere you will find him here.
But General Lee is nearer by
    At Morristown, I hear ;
He is next in rank and he will thank
    The bearer of good cheer."

To General Lee the horseman rode
    And found him, sooth to say,

At Basking Ridge, for he rode until
    It was near the break of day.
They took him in to General Lee
    Who then was in his bed;
And he gave to Lee the letter that he
    To bring had quickly sped.

"To Washington this is addressed,"
    Quoth gallant General Lee;
But Wilkinson set his mind at rest
    That it might opened be.
The seal he broke and then bespoke
    The bearer take repose;
So the messenger lay on the floor till day,
    And fell into a doze.

Rolled in his blanket warm he lay,
    The open fire before,
And took his rest among the best
    Of the General's army corps.
Now as they slumbered there and dreamed
    That distant was the foe,
A troop drew nigh led by a spy,
    As you shall shortly know.

PART III.

Till eight o'clock the General lay
    In bed, and then anon,
Half-dressed was he when he came to see
    Good Major Wilkinson.

He speaks with him in bitter words,
    For a bitter tongue has he,
Of what is done by Washington
    And those that with him be.

The precious morning hours he spends
    In wrangling with his men ;
He meets their wants with cursing taunts
    And sends them off again.
A messenger arrives who comes
    From General Sullivan
To learn the way they should take that day
    And all that should be done.

Then on a map looks General Lee
    The Princeton road to trace,
As he would lead with greatest speed
    His army to that place.
" Tell General Sullivan to march
    Toward Pluckamin," quoth he ;
" And I will come with fife and drum,
    As he shall shortly see."

Now General Lee had orders clear,
    An oft expressed command,
To join his chief right speedily
    Nor turn to either hand.
But 'tis his way to disobey
    And mar his chieftain's plan
While he starts out the foe to rout
    And be the winning man.

By this 'twas ten o'clock and now
    To breakfast they sit down,
While Sullivan goes marching on
    The road to Princeton town.
With ink and pen a letter then
    The General he must write ;
For with pen he could and often would
    Heroic words indite.

To General Gates he writes to say :—
    " There is a certain man
Who would be great in field and state
    Had he the gift of can.
But we are lost, completely lost,
    Our chief knows not the art
To beat the foe ; he is too slow
    And knows not when to start."

Just then good Major Wilkinson
    Looks out, and down the lane
He sees a troop of red-coats charge
    Upon the house amain.
" The British cavalry are here !"
    Quoth he. " O where ?" cries Lee ;
" Around the house : you are caught like a mouse,
    And that right suddenly."

" Where is the guard !" cries Lee—" the guard !
    Why don't they fire?" quoth he ;
" Where is my valiant body guard ?"
    Quoth gallant General Lee.
The guard, alas ! were off their guard,
    Their General was undone ;

Their arms they had stacked and off they
      had packed
    To bask in the winter sun.

Then the women said, " Go hide in bed !"
    This was their word to Lee :
But all in vain, for with disdain
    He scorned such strategy.
Pistol in hand then took his stand
    Good Major Wilkinson,
Prepared to shoot and fight to boot ;
    He would no foeman shun.

While thus he waits, just at the gates
    He hears a voice declare
" We'll burn the house to catch the mouse."
    'Twas then, as in despair,
That General Lee with alacrity
    Made known he did submit ;
When with a shout the soldier rout
    Compelled their man to sit
Half dressed, head bare, upon a horse,
    And off to Brunswick town
They rode away that winter's day
    With this warrior of renown.

In three hours more was heard the roar
    Of cannon from their camp ;
Loud waxed the boast of the British host
    O'er a captive of that stamp.
They thought they had our greatest man,
    The one who held the key,

In field and state, of our country's fate
　　And all our destiny.

And so we thought till we were taught
　　To thank our seeming woe,
And we learned in the end that our truest friend
　　Was the man that Lee thought was too slow.

Capt. ELIAKIM LITTELL.

JANUARY 9, 1777.

O F CAPTAIN LITTELL be my song,
　　A mighty man was he ;
And a monument that tells his fame
　　In Springfield you may see.

Upon that monument 'tis carved
　　How that he dared defy
King George the tyrant, he who thought
　　To stifle Freedom's cry.

One day the British sent a force
　　Out towards Connecticut Farms
To bring the Jerseymen to terms
　　By valiant feats of arms.

27

CAPT. ELIAKIM LITTELL.

When Captain Littell heard thereof
    He started in pursuit
And trapped that brave Waldecker band
    By strategy astute.

For in two parts he formed his men,
    The one an ambush made ;
And with the other, full in front,
    He faced them, unafraid.

" Lay down your arms at once," he cried ;
    They started to retreat,
And then, in sooth, the other band
    Of patriots they did meet.

Assailed in front, assailed in rear,
    They took the wisest course,
Laid down their arms nor fired a shot,
    That brave Waldecker force.

The British general thereat
    Was filled with rage and spite
And ordered out another force
    Of Hessians for the fight.

On came the Hessians, but the roads
    Were all to them unknown ;
While the patriot band knew every turn
    And every wall of stone.

From every vantage point they made
    Full many a sharp attack,
And, all unharmed themselves, they turned
    The troubled Hessians back.

28

Then to a swamp those Hessians fled
    To escape their deadly foe,
And there they soon laid down their arms—
    So runs the tale, I trow.

Then was that British general
    More angered than before ;
A troop of horse he ordered out
    And vengeance dire he swore.

But they in turn were put to flight,
    And being mounted men,
They fled so fast that they escaped
    And safe returned again.

Now once again the British chief
    Pursues this losing game
And bribes a tory to escort
    Three hundred men to tame

This rebel chief who dares defy
    King George and all his host ;
So quickly on their way they go
    And to his quarters post.

But not so easily entrapped
    Was Captain Littell, he
Who, as they thought, was in his house
    Pent in—for suddenly

While they prepare to charge amain
    And force their man to yield,
A troop attacks them in the rear
    And drives them from the field.

For Captain Littell, it appears
    Was not at home just then ;
Behind an old stone fence he lay
    In ambush with his men.

And when he saw the foe at hand
    He took a steady aim
And fired—the British general fell ;
    There fell his hopes of fame.

And all his followers, hard beset
    And cowering in the night
Before a foe they could not count,
    Again turned back in flight.

Now would you see the place where lies
    Brave Captain Littell's dust,
To Springfield go—his spirit now
    Is with the saints we trust.

———

    His monument is conspicuous in the Springfield Cemetery.
On it is carved:—
"CAPT. ELIAKIM LITTELL
1744–1805.
He dared to oppose George the tyrant of England an
enemy to the rights of mankind.
Springfield 1780."

A TORY.

Hanover, 1776-7.

❊❊❊❊❊❊❊❊❊❊❊❊

THERE'S a man of "consid'abul proputtee,"
 With a loftier air than you commonly see
In our plain people—an Englishman,
Who settled in Hanover,—guess if you can.
Yes; he is a Tory beyond a doubt
And is very free in "giving it out."

Full "many an ardent controversee"
Had famous Parson Green and he
On the subject of our American way
Of establishing Independence Day.
The Parson's son Ashbel oft heard
Their talk and the Tory's boastful word.

Some hot-bloods there were in Morristown
Who vowed they would "take this Tory down"
Ere his lofty airs and his high conceit
Took folks completely off their feet.
"For it is no more than right," said they ;
"Such talk as this leads folks astray."

So they gave it out that the Tory, he
With feathers and tar should coated be,
Unless in the church confession he made
Of his Toryism and promptly obeyed.
Now, you know, a word to the wise is as good
As a whole discourse half understood.

31

There's a sinner confessing in church, they say ;
Confessing his sins this Sabbath day.
'Twas Parson Green read it out this morning,
For the sinner was moved thereto by a warning
Of feathers and tar—have you heard, I say,
His full confession ?—'twas read to-day.

And then, right soon, in the afternoon,
To Morristown rode that Tory poltroon
And begged good Parson Johnes, in a flurry,
To read it again.   Quoth the parson, " No hurry !
This is not, perhaps, the time or the way ;
But actions speak louder than words, they say."

ESEK RYNO.

E SEK was a minute-man,
        Quick to act and quick to plan.
One thing the minute-man must learn
To seize the moment at the turn.
Good rule this for buckwheat cakes,
As Esek knows, for see, he takes
His griddle—breakfast time is near
And Esek is the cook, 'tis clear.
Watch your cake; ah ! that's the trick !
Turn it ere it burns ; now, quick !
Take it off!—but who comes there ?
Red-coats !   Do they want a share ?

ESEK RYNO.

They want Esek—" Come, my man ;
You're our prisoner !"   What he can
Esek does ; he makes a show
Of his loyalty ; but, no !
They are not put off ; he must
Go with them, for they mistrust
All this sudden burst of zeal
For King George ; his last appeal
Is that he may go up stairs
A moment.   Granted.   He prepares
For his journey ; but too long
He waits ; suspecting something wrong
They mount the ladder—there he stands
And plunges both his brawny hands
In a barrel of buck-wheat bran ;
Then to another barrel—" The man
Is surely hiding something !—gold
It may be !"—thus the tale is told.
They rush to the barrels, search and search
For the hidden pelf ; but in the lurch
They are left ; for Esek, the minute-man,
Is off while they explore the bran.
Down the ladder he leaped and fled,
As quick with his heels as with his head.
Half-way to the woods was he ere they
Got out of the house, nor did he stay
For the bullets that whizzed about his ears.

My story's done ; you see, it appears
That a ready wit and a barrel of bran
Are enough to save a minute-man.

33

JOHN HONEYMAN of G<small>RIGGSTOWN</small>.

✾✿✾✿✾✿✾✿✾✿✾

A ROUND the house a midnight throng
    Are clamoring, "Traitor! spy!
A spy! a tory!" and erelong,
    With firebrands flashing high,

They shout, "John Honeyman, traitor, spy,
    Come forth, or over your head
We'll burn your house in a trice!"—that cry
    Fills John's good wife with dread.

'Tis not for her husband that she fears,
    But for her children three ;
Her husband no threat of danger hears,
    For far away is he.

And well she knows that in truth he spies
    For the cause of liberty—
But the torches draw near—to the door she flies
    And forth to that mob goes she.

She waves her hand and the mob is stilled—
    " Who leads this throng, pray tell ?"
" Young Abraham Baird." Then her heart was filled
    With hopes that all would be well.

For Abraham Baird, as well she knew,
    Was a stalwart youth and brave—
" His name stands high and his heart is true ;
    My children he will save."

34

To him she called and bade him read
    A letter that she brought;
She bade him read in that hour of need
    These words with safety fraught—

"To all good people of New Jersee
    And others, be it known,
My word is given, as here you see,
    That mercy shall be shown

To John Honeyman's wife and children all,
    Though he be thought a spy;
Now let no harm their lives befall
    When this shall meet your eye."

The signature is plain to see,
    "Geo. Washington," the same
Who leads the cause of libertee,
    All honor to his name!

Then silence fell upon that throng,
    Confusion filled each breast;
And that midnight mob went home erelong,
    Young Baird among the rest.

Now when the war was at an end
    John Honeyman came back,
And the tory spy was known for a friend,
    Of friends he found no lack.

Once more the same good neighbors throng
    About his humble home;
They come to honor him who long
    Was forced afar to roam.

35

And many patriots hither came
    To see this trusty spy;
'Twas the brightest day of his new-found fame
    When Washington drew nigh.

To Lamington our hero moved
    And there in '22
He died a patriot well-approved,
    Esteemed for service true.

For he it was who through the lines
    Of the foe at Trenton came
With a secret word to aid the designs
    Of our chief and win him fame.

For the lowly life is linked with the great
    And bound to the fate of all,
And John Honeyman helped to save the state
    When its doom was like to befall.

ANNA KITCHEL'S PROTECTION.
Whippany, 1776-7.

❈❈❈❈❈❈❈❈❈❈❈

"GET a protection, Anna," quoth he,
  "'Twill keep you safe from harm;"
The Deacon he was a godly man,
  But filled with dire alarm.

" A British Protection is the thing,
  The very thing," quoth he;
" For this alone can save your life
  And all your property."

Unto the worthy Deacon then
  Thus Anna Kitchel spake,
" Protection from King George the Third
  I will not falsely take.

Is not my husband in the ranks?
  My heart with him must go;
I give no oath of fealty to
  The man he counts his foe.

My father, too, in the army serves,
  Has served for many a day;
And brothers five, if they're alive,
  Are mingling in the fray.

So now I pray to the Lord of Hosts,
  My best Protector, He;
I'll bear my share and He will care
  For me and mine," quoth she.

HUGH MERCER in the House of Burgesses.

✸✸✸✸✸✸✸✸✸✸✸✸

WHEN war, long threatened, burst upon our land;
 When, at the call of Freedom, men arose
  To arm them and to drive afar their foes,
Ambition to a sudden flame was fanned,
And patriots, eager all for high command,
 Men rich in all that Fortune's smile bestows,
 Urged each his claim; but one there was who chose
A nobler part: see yonder soldier stand,
Plain in his garb, yet with a flashing eye—
 An old-world veteran, schooled in battle's laws,
 One who with Washington hath firmly stood—
His country calls, will not he too reply?
 He writes—they read—" Mercer will serve the cause
 At any post his country may think good."

38

GENERAL MERCER at PRINCETON.

ERE MERCER fell, with bayonet-pierced breast,
    Facing his country's foes upon the field,
  Scorning to cry for quarter or to yield,
Though single-handed left and sore opprest.

He, at his chosen country's high behest,
    Was set to be a leader and to shield
    Her threatened life—with his heart's blood he sealed
That trust, nor faltered till he sank to rest.

Mourn not for him; say not untimely death
    Snatched him from fame ere we could know his worth,
    And hid the lustre of a glorious name;
Such souls go forth, when fails their vital breath,
    To shine as beacons through the mists of earth
    And kindle in men's hearts the heroic flame.

WASHINGTON at PRINCETON.

ON, to the battle's front
   Rides the undaunted chief;
On, past his quailing troops,
On, towards the charging foe ;
Halts there unmovable.

Well know his wavering men
What means that last appeal,—
" *Rally, boys, rally !*"

Full in the battle's brunt
There stands their dauntless chief
While forms the foeman's line:—

" *Ready! Aim ! Fire !*"
               —the dread
Roar of their musketry
Answers to ours,—the smoke
Hides him we love—
           O God !
Wrapped in that murky cloud
What sight awaits our gaze ?
Has he too fallen, pierced,—
Pierced by the deadly shot
Hurled in by friend and foe ?—

Ha! see—the foe is flying,
While mid the dead and dying
We hail our hero chief
Scatheless beyond belief—
" *Thank God !*"—
         " *Away, away !*
On, on ! and win the day !"

GENERAL WINDS of ROCKAWAY.

1776-7.

O HAVE you heard the General pray ?
Brave General Winds of Rockaway ;
In the Deacons' meetings that they hold
Where patriots meet, both true and bold :
'Twas there I heard him many a day,
Brave General Winds of Rockaway !

In the old, unplastered Church they met ;
No parson was there the text to set ;
But when the General once began
Loud waxed the voice of that valiant man ;
Oh yes, I've heard him many a day,
Brave General Winds of Rockaway !

In thunder tones he prayed the Lord
And fervently his name implored
To break the oppressor's yoke and free
This land, the home of liberty.
The people loved to hear him pray,
Brave General Winds of Rockaway !

And when at Chatham Bridge he stood
And faced the foe they thought it good
To take a hint that the General dropped,
So they took to their heels and never stopped ;
For he could fight as well as pray,
Brave General Winds of Rockaway !

ALEXANDER HAMILTON'S
REPORT of the ARMY.

MORRISTOWN, JANUARY 1777.

❁❁❁❁❁❁❁❁❁❁❁❁

OH, have you heard of the traitor spy ?
　　'Twas in the days of yore,
When the Arnold Tavern on the Green
　　Had opened wide its door
To gallant General Washington
　　Who turned the tide of war.

At Trenton and at Princeton, too,
　　It was our Washington
Who won a name and glorious fame
　　As ever soldier won ;
And at the Arnold on the Green
　　He stayed when all was done.

And yet for all his victories
　　Full heavy of heart was he ;
For soon he wrote, as I may quote,
　　" 'Tis plain the enemy
Know not how small our numbers, or
　　They would not let us be."

Few were his men and faint of heart,
　　And many, sad to say,
Had left their post ; his little host
　　Was like to melt away ;
No reinforcements came, although
　　Expected day by day.

42

A spy there was in his employ
    Whose place it was to hie
And mingle with the foe and so
    Bring tidings, should they try
To come this way, alack the day !
    When none to help was nigh.

Now Alexander Hamilton
    Was full of anxious care ;
Quoth he, " I see beneath it all
    A deeply hidden snare ;
For the trusted spy is an ally
    Of Howe, as I would swear."

He turned it over in his mind,
    And a deeper plot laid he ;
Quoth he, " My eye ! that traitor spy
    Is just the man for me !"
And he prepared a cunning scheme
    As you shall shortly see.

He spread his papers on his desk
    And made a long report
Of foot and horse, a splendid force,
    He counted every sort,
And named them all, both great and small,
    Nor would he cut it short.

He counted all who had left the ranks,
    And all he ever knew.
And made good work, like any clerk,
    A sight to please the view ;
When that our dwindling corporal's guard
    Had grown extremely few.

Then on a day when came that way
    The still suspected spy,
Sly Hamilton, as he would run
    Upon some errand nigh,
Slipped out and left that paper there—
    Oh he was artful sly !

For as in haste he went and said
    He would return anon ;
The traitor spy then cast his eye—
    Oh artful Hamilton !—
Along the sheet, as it was meet
    For his professi-on.

Quoth he, " In luck am I," and stuck
    The precious document
Within his pouch, as I can vouch,
    And vanished with intent
To lay his prize before the eyes
    Of Howe, to whom he went.

He showed the list to Howe who wist
    Not how to face that host ;
And kept his army closely in,
    Each soldier at his post,
Lest Washington some day should come
    And drive them from our coast.

And thus it was, that as of old
    Ulysses won the day
By cunning wiles, so Hamilton
    By first-of-April play
Entrapped the eye of that traitor spy
    And kept the foe away.

44

The POWDER MAGAZINE.

1777.

❊❊❊❊❊❊❊❊❊❊❊

WHERE Washington Hall on the Morristown Green
        Now stands, was the old-time Magazine,
Where powder and ball and muskets and all
The munitions of war were kept, I ween.

And young Jacob Ford built a mill, you know,
For making powder; 'twas just below
A sheltering hill, was that powder mill,
Where the enemy could not see it, I trow.

But a train of wagons was often seen,
With powder-casks filled, drawing near the Green ;
And with pomp and display rode a troop to convey
Those powder-casks to the Magazine.

There were spies who counted the casks that came,
And gave the foe great accounts of the same ;
But you understand, they were filled with sand,
Those powder-casks, for such was their name.

For the British were wont to try their hand
At inland raids from Staten Island ;
And it was thought good, if come they should,
They should run away with those kegs of sand.

45

EUNICE HORTON of Bottle Hill.
1776.

✿✿✿✿✿✿✿✿✿✿✿

AMONG the saints whom we should canonize
    Is Parson Horton's wife, as you shall know ;
'Tis not that she was so surpassing wise
    In theologic mysteries, although
    Her skill in learning was not mean or low,
For on her heart one text she did impress,—
" She eateth not the bread of idleness."

The parson, eke, I must immortalize
    While of his worthy spouse the deeds I show ;
A man he was, not great in fame nor size—
    Short, stout, and plain, but with a kindly glow
    Upon his countenance benign, I trow ;
His wife he loved full well and did confess
" She eateth not the bread of idleness."

His wage was scant, nor did it ever rise
    To forty pounds, but fell five pounds below ;
Yet doth his wife expedients devise
    To make both ends meet fairly, even so;
    She keeps a store, her till doth overflow ;
She buys a farm with what is in excess—
" She eateth not the bread of idleness."

Envoy.

Now all ye students who to sermonize
    At " Drew" are taught, give ear and be not slow
To heed this text ; yea, do not it despise,

For this shall keep your hearts from many a woe
   If on its application ye bestow
Your earnest thought—nor give your love the less
To her who eateth not the bread of idleness.

RUNNING the GAUNTLET.
Loantaka, February 1777.

E IGHT hundred men in line,
   Armed—not with sword and gun,
But whips, for a man must run
Three times along; in fine,
He must run the gauntlet.—" Why ?"
Why ! You haven't learned the rule.
Of this military school ;
And so, if I must reply,
I'll tell you ; but first, look !
He has started—on he flies !
And every soldier tries
To strike, though he ill can brook
To strike a comrade, yet
He has his orders.   There
Behind them everywhere
Stand officers who are set
To keep them at the task,
And so they strike ; but he
Runs past so rapidly,
They miss—what more could he ask ?

47

But he must run again,
'Tis fully a thousand feet,
And though fear makes him fleet,
He is winded ; one in ten
Of the blows that fall now light
On his bare defenceless back
And blood-stains mark his track ;
But he'll come through all right !

A third time he must try :
Weak, staggering, off he starts ;
Each blow now smites and smarts.
He falls, starts up, draws nigh
The end ; while the life-blood red
Pours downs his back—'tis done ;
The race with speed begun
Ends painful and slow.   He is led
To his hut ; the line disbands.

Why was this cruel race ?
Why all this keen disgrace ?
These are war's stern commands.
For he had left his place
In our ranks and sought to go
And join the ranks of the foe ;
Hence came this keen disgrace.

They say that he lived through it all ;
Became a trusty man ;
Lived down the terrible ban
On his manhood ; arose from that fall.

BOOK II
1777-1778

WASHINGTON at BRANDYWINE.
September 11, 1777.

✸✸✸✸✸✸✸✸✸✸✸✸

A T BRANDYWINE,—a cleared and open space;
　　Yonder, on guard, a British sentinel
　　Whose eye, alert to see if all be well,
Is fixed upon a form of manly grace,
A tall and stately form, a noble face.
　　Issuing from the copse by yonder dell,
　　That form stands forth—a presence, as they tell,
Peerless for power; but see the stranger trace
With eagle glance the British lines and mark
　　All things in sight! A sentinel should not sleep
Upon his post—up flies the sentry's gun—
　　No better marksman; he could wing a lark:
　　But now—he cannot shoot; strange tremors creep
Into his heart and save our Washington.

From VALLEY FORGE to MONMOUTH.
May 18 to June 28, 1778.

❦❦❦❦❦❦❦❦❦❦❦

THE dreary winter months of Valley Forge
 Have come and gone, the worst has been endured;
 The patriot host, to fortune's stings inured,
Prepares once more to fight the tyrant George.

In Philadelphia with strange revelry
 The Briton masquerades in grand farewell;
 Here shines the ill-starred André, and the belle
Of all that feast is one whose destiny

It is to attain a place on fame's long roll
 By taking Arnold's name, a name once bright
 With a surpassing radiance—in night
At last, alas! went down that valiant soul.

Now from the Quaker citadel the foe
 Withdraws and marches on his northward way;
 Then doth our chief pursue, intent to stay
The invading host, and strike a telling blow.

Full fifteen thousand men Sir Henry led
 And we as many, disciplined and drilled
 Through that long winter till our hearts were filled
With ten-fold daring, as we onward sped

To overtake our foes; but in our host
 Was Lee, the mischief-maker, by exchange
 Of prisoners ours again. Ah! strange, most strange
Are fate's decrees; the hearts we cherish most

Are oft-times taken from us and some wretch
    Whose kiss is poison lingers by our side.
    Great Washington, whatever may betide,
Still to the utmost doth his goodness stretch

And in the second rank of power doth place
    This treasonable, much-professing friend ;
    Then to the turning point of the field doth send
This would-be chief, this marplot—his to face

The British line and give it vigorous check
    Until our chief should come and put to rout
    The British force ; but Lee, self-willed, doth flout
The thought of following orders—nay, he'll wreck

The whole campaign and let the foeman win.
    Wayne shall not charge, but only make a feint ;
    And while Wayne chafes beneath this strange
        restraint,—
" Back, Lafayette !" the order comes, " 'tis sin

To think that our mean troops can hope to stand
    Against the British regulars ; back, retreat !"
    Then Lafayette sends off a rider fleet
To Washington to say, " Best be at hand ;

Something's afoot far other than you meant."
    Our men, that torrid Sunday late in June,
    Were eager for the fray, but one poltroon
May start a panic, the enthusiasm is spent

With which we faced the foe when first we met ;
    Retreat is sounded; backward roll our ranks
    In dire confusion, when—to God be thanks !
Up rides our great commander, visage set

53

In awful wrath—to Lee, " What means all this ?"
    At that fierce tone and look the traitor quailed.
    Again that word, more fierce; the traitor paled
With anger; made complaint with cowardly hiss

That he was given a task too hard ; in fact,
    His plan was different ; 'twas not quite the thing
    To charge the foe incontinently and bring
Upon our heads a general fight—rash act !"

" Your plan !" exclaimed his chief in sharp reproof;
    " Obey your orders !" Swift he wheels about
    To turn our men, snatch victory from rout
And bids Lee from the conflict keep aloof.

Now, stern Steuben, thy work shall save the day!
    These men, long-drilled, though now in full retreat,
    Form at the word and wheel about and meet
The advancing foe, and give him cause to stay.

Off rides our chief, brings up his army all.
    Greene's battery opens fire ; Wayne full in front
    Attacks the foe, who bravely bear the brunt
Of battle's onset, but must backward fall.

Steuben is summoned, still two miles behind.
    Lee, sulking still, waylays him, bids him halt—
    " There's some mistake, some one must be at fault ;
It cannot be !—advance ? You must be blind!

The foe are there ! Retreat, I say ; retreat !"
    The sturdy baron heeds him not—but see !
    The British turn, they turn ; they flee, they flee !
Night quells the raging fires of battle's heat.

And in that night Sir Henry, taught of old,
    Withdraws his force,—is off to Middletown.
    Though questioned be the meed of high renown
Won on this day, yet can we well uphold

Our claim to vantage gained ; our leader's plan
    Was foiled by shameless, open treachery.
    Next day Lee writes; demands apology
From Washington, " that rash, hot-tempered man."

Blind to his duty, to his error blind,
    The traitor Lee is tried by martial court,
    And stripped of his rank ; here end his hopes, in short :
Ambitious to be first, left far behind !

And as the page of history we scan,
    A letter, long-forgotten, comes to view,
    Which tells the worst we feared, but never knew,
The double-dealing of that treacherous man.

" Hold, friend ! your story's incomplete ; be it known
    Lee pled his case with apt ability,
    Showed cause for his action." Yes, that history
Is known to me ; but did you mark the tone

Of insolence in Lee's perpetual sneers ?
    Forever carping at his leader's deeds,
    Forever sowing broadcast evil seeds
Of discontent ? One thing at least appears :

Had Washington been cast in meaner mold,
    Quick to descend into that petty strife
    Of wrangling words ; had not his noble life
Been as a shield, thus had the tale been told :

FROM VALLEY FORGE TO MONMOUTH.

Our guardian host, with spiteful discord riven,
    Is cleft in twain ; each faction fierce to uphold
    Its favorite leader ; while the zeal grows cold
That erst with patriotic warmth had striven

To save our cause : the people of the land,
    Blind to all else, take sides in the dispute ;
    Our cause, so weak, now dying at the root,
Would wither soon, and the oppressor's hand

Bear sway—O unpropitious, fatal hour !
    Such is the secret of full many a fall,
    When thrones have toppled ; when no clarion call
Rings out to rouse the nation to the power

That lies in pure, devoted loyalty
    To one, great worthy leader—where is one
    Who bears the palm from our own Washington,
So tried, so true, from every stain so free ?

SAMUEL PIERSON of the LIFE GUARD.
PART I.
AT CHAD'S FORD, SEPTEMBER 11, 1777.

❀❀❀❀❀❀❀❀❀❀❀

" THE battle is on us ; here, Pierson, your chief
    Has sent for you." Pierson in haste
Reports. "These despatches—no moment to waste—
Bear these to the river ; in brief,

Wait there on the bank ; from the opposite side
    Will cross such a man as I say ;
    Meet him—give him these." Then swift on his way
Rode Pierson, his good steed astride.

Of the famous life-guard he was one, a true man ;
    Athletic, a horseman expert ;
    But heedless a trifle, for see him pervert
His orders ; a moment to scan

The opposite bank he has paused ; well and good ;
    Sees no one, and then with a dash
    Plunges in, swims his horse—don't you see ? he is rash ;
On the bank he should longer have stood.

For who knows ! in the bush may lurk hidden the foe,
    A shot may unseat him ; then, too,
    His man was to cross ; 'tis the wrong thing to do,
For Pierson to cross. Does he know

If he were entrapped and his letter should fall
    In the hands of the foe, what 'twould mean ?
    It may mean defeat, for some move unforeseen
May ruin his chieftain and all.

But his man has emerged from the bush and prepares
    To cross in a boat as agreed ;
    With that, Pierson turns to the boat his good steed,
Throws over despatches, and fares

Swift back to Headquarters ; reports " All is well."
    Next morning five soldiers are sent
    By the chief-in-command to the brave Pierson's tent ;
He must march under guard, sad to tell.

Said his chief : " You have disobeyed orders my man."
    " How so ?" answered he, " At the risk
    Of my life I rode forth, and was there in the whisk
Of a lamb's tail ; no better I can."

Said his chieftain, " I told you to wait on the bank
    Till some one should cross to your side ;
    But you plunged in the stream with your horse ; this
        was wide
Of the mark ; but good fortune's to thank

That your horse was not seen as you swam to the shore,
    And no foeman was lurking to track
    The other who with those despatches went back,
For then had our cause suffered sore."

Then down on his knee went Pierson and cried,
    " I see it ! I see it ! now, pray,
    Grant me pardon this once and I'll strictly obey
Your orders when next I am tried."

" I grant it," said he ; but lay this well to heart—
    If again such offense be made known,
    It will cost you far dearer the fault to atone ;
Mind your finish as well as your start."

PART II.

AT MONMOUTH, JUNE 28, 1778.

The battle of Monmouth is now at its height
    And Pierson is called on again,
    To bear a despatch from his chief to the men
Who are far on the edge of the fight.

'Twas a perilous ride, for he had but one way,
    Direct where the fire of the foe
    In a murderous hail-storm was poured—would he go ?
He is off, in the thick of the fray.

A cannon-ball strikes his good steed and it falls—
    " Despatches !" he cries, " A fresh steed !"
    Remounts in an instant and flies at full speed
Through the hail-storm of death-dealing balls.

Again his horse fell and the man was held fast
    By the corpse of the steed where it lay ;
    But on a third horse he was set, so they say,
And rode to the finish at last.

And when to the view of his chief he returned,
    " How fared those despatches ?" Then he—
    " Delivered as ordered." " Ah ! Pierson, I see
The pardon I gave is well earned.

How fared you ? Has none of that murderous hail
    The way to your gallant heart found ?"
    " Two horses fell, shot ; I was pinned to the ground—
On the third I got through without fail."

" Well done !" said his chief ; " brave Pierson ; well done !
    And warmly I praise you to-day
    For that perilous ride through the thick of the fray,
As well finished, thank God, as begun !"

An Incident at the BATTLE of MONMOUTH.
June 28, 1778.

WHAT warrior rides so fast on his way
    To turn the tide of war this day ?
I hear the beat of his horse's feet
As he comes this way mid the terrible heat
Of this June Sabbath in Monmouth town,
When our army must fight the British crown.

Our men are fleeing, they say ! Could I go
To the battle-field I would let them know
What a woman can do – but nearer now
That horseman comes ; yes, I see how
I can do my part for the cause to-day,
Though far from the battle I must stay.

The rider draws rein—'tis Washington,
He has heard that our men are on the run ;
He can pause but a moment to quaff the cup
That a woman's hand is passing up
To refresh his heart in the hour of need
And bid him ride on with a hearty " God-speed !"

He leans from the saddle, she hears him say,
In tones subdued, ere he rides away,—
" Madam, God only knows if I
Shall drink another"—she sees him fly
To the scene of war, where the hail of death
Falls thick about him ; with bated breath
Men watch for his fall, but God's angels shield
Our leader once more on that battle-field.

GATES and WASHINGTON.

1777-80.

✶✶✶✶✶✶✶✶✶✶✶

GATES with his northern laurels crowned, admired
　　And flattered to the full, looks down in pride
Upon his chief so often foiled, denied
The meed of victory, though none more inspired
With patriotic zeal to do and dare,
To achieve the utmost, fate's worst stings to bear.

But twice of late, at Brandywine, again
At Germantown, he has failed of the renown
That victory yields, the bright, invisible crown
That makes a leader glorious, fires his men
With high enthusiasm, doubles each blow
And with dire panic smites the trembling foe.

" Ah, well! no man can flee his destiny ;
All is, we mortals must keep watch and know
Whose star is rising, whose descending low."
So Conway thought and his astrology
Made Gates the star which should fulfill our hopes
And cheer the land that now in darkness gropes.

In secret session Congress hesitates
Between two courses—shall they put aside
Their patriot chief, long-trusted, true and tried ?
By factions rent, the fickle throng awaits
The turn of fortune that shall yet bestow
The chief command on Gates, whose star they know.

GATES AND WASHINGTON.

But Monmouth adds new lustre to the name
Of Washington, and Southern willows crown
Gates' head once filled with hopes of high renown.
A broken-hearted man, exposed to shame,
Is Gates ; bereaved as well, he deeply mourns
His son ; the laurels now are changed for thorns.

While, bowed with grief, he never thinks to know
Another joy, come words of sympathy
From him he had wronged by scheming jealousy
And sought by unworthy arts to overthrow ;
These tender words now steal his grief away
Till o'er his darkness dawns a new-found day.

For he hath learned the secret of that might
Wherein his chief is great, and from afar
He greets the rising brightness of the star
That soon shall glow with heaven's undoubted light
And shine with beaming, ever-brightening ray—
Our country's morning star, fadeless for aye.

BOOK III
1778-1779

The MIDDLEBROOK WINTER CAMP.

1778-79.

⚜✾✾✾✾✾✾✾✾✾✾✾

'TWAS in December of seventy-eight
  That Washington marched through
On his way to camp at Middlebrook Heights
  Where he may keep in view

New Brunswick and the road that leads
  From Staten Island down
To Philadelphia, ready thus
  To check the British crown

In any move by land to the South,
  Or, should they northward go,
He too could move his troops that way
  Nor would they find him slow.

Here Lady Washington set wide
  Her hospitable door
And dames and damsels fair to see
  Were counted by the score.

A mild and open season this,
  The cold was not severe;
By April first the trees were in bud
  And signs of spring were clear.

Our men were in high feather all,
 And proud of Monmouth fight ;
Well drilled were they, their hearts were gay
 And now they took delight

In balls and grand reviews and all
 The pomp of dress parade ;
While Cupid's darts assailed some hearts
 And deadly havoc made.

GENERAL KNOX.

AT PLUCKAMIN brave General Knox
 Encamped the gunner corps
On rising ground beside the road
 And here was seen great store

Of mortars, howitzers in line,
 And heavy cannon; some
Were spoils of war and from Burgoyne
 Far in the North had come.

In coats of black turned up with red
 The artillery corps were clad ;
And hats with yellow trimmed they wore
 And breeches white they had.

Jacobus Van der Veer it was
 With whom Knox made his home
And Dame Knox with her husband shared
 Wherever he might roam.

The General was a genial man
    Of presence passing grand,
His manly voice made all rejoice
    And well he could command.

His wife was the heroine of our camp,
    Vivacious, dignified ;
Of a noble mind nor could you find
    A pair more satisfied.

Portly was he and she was stout,
    They were a jovial pair ;
A fond and happy pair were they
    And yet they had their share

Of sorrow in this life, for here
    An infant child they lost ;
Nor this alone ; but, first and last,
    Seven died—such was the cost

Of war's hard life with all the train
    Of stress and strain it brings ;
Those times tried strong men's souls—too hard
    Were they for weak, wee things.

And now a strange, unhappy scene
    Was here to see ; forsooth,
The church at Pluckamin was Dutch
    And held it gospel truth

That none of other creeds could lie
    Within the sacred ground
Where pious Dutchmen lay ; for such
    A burial must be found

67

Outside the consecrated bounds ;
    And so when there was need
For Knox to lay his dead away,
    As he was of the creed

That in New England did prevail,
    These pious men must spurn
His quest for burial of his child
    And bid him elsewhere turn.

'Twas then Jacobus Van der Veer
    Was deeply moved, for he
Had suffered in like manner from
    This cruel bigotry.

He too had lost a child and she,
    Though born within the bound
Of the true church, as they believed,
    Was barred from holy ground.

For she was one whose clouded mind.
    With darkness overcast,
Knew not the joy of reason's light,
    And when she died, at last,

They said, " We know not if she be
    Among the saved, 'tis clear
She could not know her Lord above,
    She did not know him here."

And so her father laid her dust
    In a field beyond the line
That shut God's Acre in for those
    Who would its bounds define.

And now Jacobus Van der Veer
 With tenderness was touched;
His voice it was half choked with sobs,
 The General's hand he clutched,

And led him to a field were lay
 His own afflicted child,
Outside the fence, mute evidence
 Of a soul from heaven exiled.

" Here, Gen'ral, lay your baby here,"
 Said he; and it was done.
So there they lie, but the fence has been changed
 And takes them in, each one.

FRIEDRICH WILHELM AUGUSTUS, BARON VON STEUBEN.

INSPECTOR–GENERAL Steuben
 It was who here did drill
Our troops, as erst at Valley Forge
 To do their leader's will.

By daily exercise and drill,
 Inspections and reviews,
He taught our rustic soldiery
 How best their arms to use.

BARON STEUBEN.

He scrutinized each soldier's dress,
    Each gun in hand he took,
And if one speck of rust he found
    'Twas more than he could brook.

Of temper stern and quick was he,
    Yet of a kindly heart ;
And when he stormed at his awkward troops
    'Twas taken in good part.

He saw we had the making of
    Good soldiers, and he drilled
From morn till night until in place
    Of rustic ways he instilled

The warlike arts that had won the day
    On many a battle-field
For Frederick the Great,—to us
    A new world he revealed.

Oft had the British regulars
    Made merry when they caught
Some rustic specimen of our troops,
    Un-uniformed, untaught.

Of such a one they asked what he
    Could do—mid loud deridings ;
" I flank a little now and then,"
Quoth he, " and carry tidin's."

Their bayonets our soldiers lost
    Or used as spits for roasting ;
But thanks to stern Steuben they soon
    Of Stony Point were boasting.

BARON STEUBEN.

The Baron was a stately man
    And glorious in array,
With gold and diamonds and stars
    Remembered many a day

By those who saw him on parade
    At the head of his army corps ;
Of martial aspect he, and looked
    A very " god of war."

Long had he served on foreign fields,
    Won place and honors high ;
And high rewards—all these he left
    And came as an ally

To help our continental host,
    In hopes a field to find
Where he might win a lasting fame,
    More than he left behind.

Nor was his hope in vain, for here
    He learned to fight the fight
Of Freedom, saw men fight because
    They loved their land—their might

Was more than military art
    And more than studied rules
That strategists and martinets
    E'er taught in warlike schools.

He taught us much, we taught him more,
    And here he won great fame
And a home in the hearts that long will love
    The brave old Baron's name.

Colonel ALEXANDER SCAMMEL.

FULL six feet two the Colonel stood,
  A goodly man was he,
With a great warm heart in his manly breast,
  No truer man could be.

A tender heart was his, but strong
  And stern to keep in check
Whate'er might harm the right or tend
  To bring our cause to wreck.

But there were some high in our ranks
  Who from the cause did swerve
When Cupid's arts ensnared their hearts
  The British crown to serve.

Now Colonel Scammel loved a maid,
  In Mystic she did dwell ;
For years he had been courting her,
  'Twas known he loved her well.

But she avowed she would not wed
  A warrior who fought
Upon the bloody battle-field
  And deeds of horror wrought.

In vain the Colonel urged his suit,
  In vain besought some word
Of consolation for his woe ;
  His pleading was unheard.

72

She would not be his bride except
 On one condition—this
That he should leave the army, thus
 And only thus find bliss.

At last good Colonel Scammel, torn
 By feelings strong and deep,
Chose Freedom for his bride and pledged
 His sword her vows to keep.

'Twas here at Middlebrook he won
 That victory o'er his heart,
Gave up the maid, and thus he played
 A true heroic part.

And two years later on the field
 They found this soldier brave,
Laid low by a deadly wound that brought
 His great heart to the grave.

AT THE BALL.

Given at Pluckamin, in Honor of the French
Alliance, February 18, 1779.

"THE fiddles have ceased for a moment and now
 Let me ask you, my charming Miss Linn, if you
 please,
Do you not feel disturbed and somewhat ill at ease—
I hope you will frankly and freely avow

73

The genuine truth—do you not, as I say,
    When a leonine roar through the ball-room, perchance,
    Is heard o'er the hubbub of music and dance—
Do you not feel depressed, though it sounds far away ?"

" O no, not at all," she replies, " for you see
    It rather enlivens the scene, don't you know ;
    Such creatures howl loudest—you know it is so—
When they are most frightened and ready to flee."

" And do you not think ?" added she, " you who know
    So much more than we girls, that this lion may dread
    The mighty Armada of Spain ?   It is said
That the monarch of Spain—but his movements are slow—

Will acknowledge our cause, though he smiles on John Bull."
    " So," said I, " you suppose that the King of Spain acts
    In affairs of this kind—to compare with known facts—
As do ladies, who smile on a man till he's full

Of anticipations of happiness, then
    Entangle his steps till, tied fast to a wife,
    He finds himself captured and shackled for life."
" At what age, pray," the fair one replies, " do you men

Cease paying such compliments ?"   Then, as she smiled,
    A tall figure approached in a black velvet suit
    And dispelled her arch glance by a stately salute,
And thus I was saved ere my heart she beguiled.

But who is the partner who now holds her hand?
    With a nobleman's grace and grave mien, high aloft
    He clasps in his own that small hand, fair and soft,
And walks through the dance, imperturbable, grand.

He wears knee-buckles, shoe-buckles, rapier of steel ;
   With his hair, thickly powdered, drawn back and held in
   By a black silken bag—and the favored Miss Linn
Marches proudly with him through the old-fashioned reel.

Who is he? Look twice, if in truth at first sight
   You know not the man who late braved the fierce fire
   Of the British at Monmouth, and blazing with ire
Snatched fame from defeat—there he dances to-night!

And long will the fair ones of Pluckamin tell
   How this one and that one was led to the dance
   By that tall, stately figure who rivets the glance
Of all in the room—yes, his name you know well.

The GRAND REVIEW at Bound Brook, May 2, 1779.

I.

'TWAS in seventy-nine on the second of May,
   When old Bound Brook saw a glorious sight ;
Such pageantry, pomp, and brilliant display !
   Such high dignitaries and ladies bedight
With gayest of colors, bright banners afloat
   On the breath of the breeze, all the people astir,
The gentry marked out by the cut of the coat—
   Such bustle, such grandeur, I'm bound to aver
Are not to be seen in these days, you may laugh,
These days of the trolley and telautograph.

II.

These grand jubilations are all from regard
    To the envoys of Europe, now with us, you know ;
The envoy of France is here, Monsieur Gerard,
    On whom young and old their first glances bestow,
For he comes from the land of our noble allies,
    The land of Vergennes, Beaumarchais, Lafayette,
And all look upon him with wondering eyes—
    The envoy of France !   But we must not forget
Don Juan de Miralles, the envoy from Spain,
Just arrived from Havana the news to obtain.

III.

There are grand preparations and crowds throng the place,
    All out for a gala day ; see the grand stand
In the midst of yon field !   There fair ladies grace
    The day with their presence ; there, first in the land,
You may see Lady Washington, and by her side
    Two young lady visitors, real F. F. V.'s,
Meaning Fair From Virginia, as we may decide ;
    And near them is seated a dame who with ease
Might pass for an empress, Dame Knox, who but she ?
As grand as a queen, and as good, all agree.

IV.

And there, see the wife of brave General Greene ;
    She's the belle of the day—young, lovely, and gay ;
Her gray eyes lit up by a mind that is keen
    To observe all about her and then store away
What she sees, and at last bring it forth to delight
    All hearts with the converse that charms by its spell.

Sought after is she, but I haste to recite
    My story ; the fact is I hardly dare tell
The charms of the fair ones who came here to see
And be seen, to be sure, but one thing we are free

V.

To conclude, and that is that the Stocktons were there
    From Princeton ; and then from Elizabeth Town,
The Livingstons, surely, and Clarks ; and a share
    Of this glory was due to that name of renown,
Lord Stirling of Basking Ridge; likewise the Lotts
    Of famed Morristown—from all parts of the state
The people poured in until, gayest of spots,
    Old Bound Brook was filled with the fair and the great ;
But now 'tis a quieter place with no hint
Of that scene once so gay with each bright rainbow tint.

VI.

O could you have seen them, those gentry of old,
    The elders with flat-bottomed wigs, still in vogue ;
While the young and more stylish, as I have been told,
    Wore their hair in a queue—'twas Sir Joshua, the rogue,
Who said that a gentleman dressed in the style
    And a Cherokee Indian seemed on a par,
And whichever, on meeting, should first dare to smile
    At the other, e'en though it should be from afar,
He might well be esteemed the barbarian still,
In all else alike save control of the will.

VII.

And now at this pageant, the old stately ways
    Of colonial times the beholder may note ;

THE GRAND REVIEW.

See yon young gallant, upon him fix your gaze,
　　A cocked hat 'neath the arm of his many-hued coat—
Knee-breeches, striped stockings of silk, pointed shoes
　　With buckles that shine as he bows at the door
Of a lumbering coach—nay, look ! do not lose
　　One action ; what grave, ceremonious lore
These youngsters must learn ! See, he hands the fair maid
To a seat on the stage whence the field is surveyed.

VIII.

But ere she is seated she turns to salute
　　Her stately gallant with a curtsey well-aimed,
Sinking low to the ground ; whereupon this recruit
　　In the ranks of Dame Grundy, this savage reclaimed,
With hat heavy-laced raised in air, bows in turn,
　　Waves his leg, scrapes the floor (or the ground) with
　　　　his boot,
And then—all is over ; but come, let us learn
　　What this noise is about ; some new move is afoot ;
Let us mount the grand-stand and observe the display
Of war with its legions in brilliant array.

IX.

Now salvos of cannon announce to the throng
　　That our chieftains draw near with the guests of the day ;
A bright cavalcade, on they come and erelong
　　We see at their head Harry Lee—tell me, pray,
Saw you ever a handsomer troop than he leads,
　　This brave Captain Lee ? In white and in green
His legion is clad and superb are their steeds.
　　With plumes nodding gaily, a holiday scene,
They prance by the stand ; sabres clank, jangle spurs—
Our pets ! and the sight every heart deeply stirs.

78

x.

And now the commander-in-chief comes in sight;
    All eyes turn to him—see him, calm, dignified,
A grave, stately presence, in nobleness quite
    The peer of a king—nay, I think, by his side
No crowned head of Europe would equal our chief
    In power to impress every heart with such awe
And such genuine loyalty, from the belief
    Of his unswerving goodness, as true as God's law.
He believed in our cause, he believed in our land;
King over himself, he had right to command.

XI.

Not quite fifty years have passed over his head
    As we see it to-day 'neath that three-cornered hat;
And the soldierly form that so often has led
    Our troops to the fray, where the balls fall pat-pat,
Now, arrayed in full uniform, sits his bright bay
    With a grace unsurpassed; see the buff and the blue,
Those epaulets, boots, all that goodly display!
    That ivory sword-hilt! Ah, yes, but the view
That charms us the most is the look of the man,
The face that all present are eager to scan.

XII.

And now come the generals all and their staffs;
    There is Greene, tall and manly, intelligent, wise;
Not yet thirty-seven years old, but he quaffs
    The cup of his leader's best love—in the eyes
Of Washington this is the man who could best
    Succeed to his post, should mishap, woe the day!
Remove him from service; events well attest
Greene's clear-headed wisdom and none can gainsay

The brave Quaker's skill in the soldier's rude art ;
But, though master of war, he loves peace in his heart.

XIII.

Next comes the big-hearted and merry-eyed Knox,
    A favorite with all, and of him you have heard ;
Then brave Muhlenberg, once a parson, and Wayne
    Whom the people, who often will give in a word
Their idea of a man, dub " The Dandy" ; again
    He is nick-named " Mad Anthony." Now you may see
All glittering with proud decorations, Steuben.
    And there rides a stripling, distinguished is he
For his clear, brilliant intellect ; he can afford
To rest his best fame on the pen, not the sword.

XIV.

Don Juan de Miralles among them is seen
    In a suit of bright crimson with gold aiguilette,
And the envoy from France comes riding between
    In a rich broidered coat, decked with jewels, and yet
The splendor and pageantry is but begun ;
    Hear the rat-a-tat-tat and the boom-boom-de-ay
Of the soul-stirring drums, while arms glint in the sun ;
    See the trappings and glory of warlike array !
Hear the ear-piercing fife and the trumpet's loud blare !
On they go, past the stand, while huzzahs fill the air.

XV.

Then the regiments draw up in line on the field
    And the officers pass and repass in review
With salutes in due order ; at last the chiefs yield
    The day to the men of the line, who go through

Their maneuvers and all evolutions of war
    Till at last they pass by with the marching salute.
Flags waving and pennons a-flutter, each corps
    Sweeps by in quick time and we here see the fruit
Of the Baron's stern lessons ; each man marches by
Proud to feel the keen glance of his chief's eagle eye.

XVI.

What glad acclamations ! as cheer after cheer
    Rings out from that throng who are gathered to see ;
While those men, once a mark for the jibe and the jeer
    Of Red-coats and tories, march by gallantly.
Among them are men who once shivered with cold
    On that dread winter night when to Trenton they
        crossed ;
At Brandywine others have bled ; once enrolled
    In these ranks were the forms of brave fellows who lost
Their lives in the fierce fight of Monmouth—let not
Their share in these ringing huzzahs be forgot.

The BANQUET.

XVII.

THEN the chiefs and their staffs, and perchance a few more,
    With the noteworthy guests of the day, mounted horse
And away through the village they rode, full three score
    In the party, prepared, a redoubtable force,
To do execution upon the repast
    That Steuben at his quarters has spread 'neath the trees

In honor of Monsieur Gerard. Here at last
    The hospitable Baron puts all at their ease ;
A well-beloved host was the Baron and none
Was more ready to please when his drilling was done.

XVIII.

And ably assisted was he on this day
    By the clever young men who long served on his staff ;
Pierre Duponceau, the young Frenchman so gay,
    Only nineteen years old, always ready to laugh,
Was among them ; from France he had come as the scribe
    Of the Baron ; and yet, of the lovers of fun
And all the mirth-makers, that jovial tribe
    Who lighten life's burdens, there surely was none
More merry than young Captain Fairlie, whose art
Even stirred to light laughter our staid leader's heart.

XIX.

Nor must I pass over the good William North,
    As dear to the Baron, 'tis said, as a son ;
In camp, in the field, both now and henceforth,
    Their friendship grew stronger ; and still there is one
To be named in this group, Captain Walker, who knew
    Both tactics and French—have you heard of the way
Steuben wrote his book ?—'tis too good to be true.
    'Twas the book upon tactics ; Steuben as they say,
First wrote it in German, then turned it about
Into French that a native-born Frenchman would scout.

XX.

Then his aides took it up ; Fleury bettered the French
    And then, in poor English, the gay Duponceau,
Just landed from France, did his utmost to quench
    The last spark of meaning that yet dared to glow

Through the mists of these languages; then to correct
   The work of these scholars, 'twas taken in hand
By Walker—Steuben, at the last, could detect
   No glimpse of its meaning; and so our brave band
Was drilled in three tongues and successively cursed
In French, German, English, whiche'er sounded worst.

XXI.

And now, to do honor to Monsieur Gerard,
   An old friend of the Baron's in Europe and still
Attached by firm ties of unbroken regard,
   These gay cavaliers went to work with a will
To meet the occasion.   With many a quip
   They tickled the fancy and rose to each toast,
" There's many a slip 'twixt the cup and the lip,"
   Said Monsieur Gerard, " but, I hope, my dear host,
That the happy alliance established between
Fair France and America yet shall be seen

XXII.

To result in success to the cause you espouse."
   Then young Captain Fairlie was called on, and said,
" The words of our much-esteemed envoy arouse
   Glad thoughts in my mind, I assure you ;" then led
By looks of expectancy, cries of " Hear !   Hear !"
   He spoke of the glorious alliance, the hopes
That it brought, lighting up all our darkness with cheer ;
   And then after gracefully rambling along,
   He brought his remarks to a close with this song :—

An EARNEST of VICTORY.

AIR: *Vive la Compagnie.*

THERE was a young Frenchman came over the sea,
    Over the storm-tossed sea!
His name was Pi-erre, he'd a gay, winsome air
That always takes well with the young and the fair—
    Over the storm-tossed sea.

He came with the Baron, good Baron Steuben,
    Over the storm-tossed sea;
He'd a cheek like a peach, and was ready of speech
With French or with English to fill up the breach—
    Over the storm-tossed sea.

A wager he laid as he sailed o'er the sea,
    Over the storm-tossed sea;
That the first Yankee girl he should meet on the street,
He would kiss her, he would; and he vowed that he could—
    Over the storm-tossed sea.

'Twas a bright, frosty day when he first came ashore
    Over the storm-tossed sea;
Clear and and keen was the air, when this gay young Pierre,
Stepped up to a maiden, a maiden so fair—
    Over the storm-tossed sea.

Then gravely he bowed and declared he had come
    Over the storm-tossed sea;
And left his own land to strengthen the band
That fight for America's rights, understand—
    Over the storm-tossed sea.

AN EARNEST OF VICTORY.

·" And as I was sailing the billows," quoth he,
　　" Over the storm-tossed sea ;
I thought it were sweet on the threshold to meet
Some fair one, in sooth, who the wanderer would greet—
　　Over the storm-tossed sea.

And should she agree, when I sail o'er the sea,
　　Over the storm-tossed sea,
To vouchsafe me a kiss—pray don't take it amiss—
'Twere an omen of good to my errand, I wis,
　　Over the storm-tossed sea."

So spake the young Frenchman who sailed o'er the sea,
　　Over the storm-tossed sea,
And his prayer met success, as well you may guess,
For the Puritan maiden, she could but say " Yes"—
　　Over the storm-tossed sea !

XXXIII.

As the last note was sung, they all cried, " A good hit !"
　　For the story was known, and the gay Duponceau
Was there to attest it, and could but admit,
　　When called on to respond, that the facts were just so ;
·" And the pleasant success of that day," exclaimed he,
　　" When a wanderer and stranger, I first stepped ashore,
After sailing so long on the tempest-tossed sea,
　　Gives me hope that this tedious and troublesome war
Will yet have as happy and pleasing an end
As the song we have heard from the lips of our friend."

A Ballad of MILLSTONE.

THE British have come,
  Tant–a–ra! drum, drum!
The British have come to Millstone.

Why have they come?
Tant–a–ra! drum, drum!
Why have they come to Millstone?

For mischief, no doubt;
All the men cleared out
When the British came into Millstone.

All the men ran away;
One old woman, they say,
Awaited the British in Millstone.

They said, " If you please,
Hand over your keys,"
The British who came into Millstone.

And they said, " 'Tis our pleasure
You tell where your treasure
Is hid"—when they visited Millstone.

But her keys she held fast
Till they wearied at last,
The British who came into Millstone.

The house they ransacked,
But of plunder they lacked,
Those soldiers who came into Millstone.

Then brutal they grew
When she gave them no clue,
Those warriors who came into Millstone.

And they hung her, head down,
Those knights of the crown,
Those chivalrous Britons at Millstone.

And left her to die,
But the neighbors drew nigh
When the red-coats had gone out of Millstone.

And she was released
Ere her heart-beat had ceased,
When the British departed from Millstone.

She was black in the face,
But more black the disgrace
Of the British who came into Millstone.

The BATTLE of MINISINK.

July 22, 1779.

EIGHTY men in the wilderness,
　　Battling hard for their lives ;
Five hundred are their foes
　　With muskets and scalping knives.
Fierce is the hail of death
　　That falls on the martyr band ;
Dark is the pall of horror
　　That settles over the land.

THE BATTLE OF MINISINK.

Who is this terrible foe?
   Brandt and his fiendish crew;
Indians half, half tories:
   'Tis but two days since they slew
The NEVERSINK victims—all gory
   The fresh scalps dangle in view.
These are the savage allies
   Of the mother-country—mad demons!
Pitiless!   In such wise
   She seeks to subdue her children.

Eighty men in the wilderness
   Battling hard for their lives;
Five hundred are their foes
   With muskets and scalping knives.
Fiercely the battle is waged
   In that wild ravine of the mountains;
Closely the patriot band is caged
   Between hillside and forest;
Shoulder to shoulder they fight,
   Beset by the sons of the forest;
Bravely they battle and smite
   The painted foe in the bushes;
Fiercely their fire is returned
   And the angel of death swift rushes
Into the patriot ranks
   And reaps a glorious harvest.

Falling! falling! their flanks
Are exposed to the blazing muskets;
One by one they drop in their tracks—
Look yonder! a soldier

Tall and stalwart of frame,
Daniel Tallmadge by name,
Leaps high in air and falls ;
One of the flying balls
Has pierced his heart and he falls.

And yonder ! behind that rock
Stands a patriot, pouring the death–fire
Into the ranks of the foe,
Holding their line in check, for they know
How deadly his aim ; but his gun grows hot—
Yonder's an idle gun !
From his rock he rushes to gain
The coveted weapon ; the shot
Patters about him like rain,
But it smites him not.

'Tis Moses DeWitt, and bravely he fought
Till his musket failed him, and safely he brought
A wounded comrade out of the reach
Of the fiendish screech
That curdles the blood.

And here on the battle's edge,
Beneath a sheltering ledge
Is Colonel Tustin, who strives
By the art of the healer to save
These men who have proved themselves brave
At the peril of their lives.

" Let the brave men follow me !
      Cowards may stay behind !"
Such was the cry that day
      Of Major Meeker, as he

Dashed ahead—by that taunt made blind,
Madly they rushed on their way,
Brave men, but alas! too few,
In pursuit of Brandt and his crew.
Prudence they cast to the wind,
Deigning not to obey
Tustin and Hathorn the wary,
Their leaders true—but the adversary
Has broken the ranks of the patriot-band,
Where with clubbed muskets they stand;
Powder and ball have failed and the end
Of the fight is at hand;
To the storm they bend
And flee for their lives—
But the wounded!
Under that rocky ledge,
Just on the battle's edge,
Each heart is throbbing, each ear
Alert, as the foe draws near.
Nearer and nearer still
Sounds that dread, blood-curdling whoop!
" O God!—thy will be done !"
Cry the helpless.   The savage troop
Is upon them.   Too weak to shun
The hatchet and scalping knife,
They are massacred, every one !
Nights puts an end to the strife.

Eighty men in the wilderness;
    Forty are wounded to death.
Fallen are some, and some

In the forest shall draw their breath,
Their last breath, under the stars,
Under the stars to-night.

Brave men these! let a monument stand
    To honor the fallen.
Brave men these! let a peaceful land
    Remember the fallen.

LIGHT HORSE HARRY at PAULUS HOOK.

August 19, 1779.

✿✿✿✿✿✿✿✿✿

Victosque armis humanitate devinxit.

O HARRY LEE it was who did
    A daring deed one day
And Congress had a medal struck
    To tell his fame for aye.

Now would you hear about that deed,
    Attend my humble song,
And I will tell as best I may
    That tale, 'twill not be long.

For well we may, at this far day,
    Recall each worthy deed
Wrought by the men who battled then
    To meet their country's need.

At Paulus Hook there was of old
    A military post,
Where Jersey City now is seen
    And the British made their boast

That none could take that citadel
    With ramparts strong begirt ;
So strong it was the garrison
    Grew careless to their hurt.

For Captain Lee one summer's day
    Led forth a chosen band
Three hundred strong, and Stirling sent
    A part of his command.

From Bergen marched this troop by night
    Unto the Hackensack,
Full fourteen miles below the Hook,
    And here Lee took the track

Among the hills and reached ere morn
    The point that was his aim ;
Through the loose-barred gate he entered straight
    And won his way to fame.

The sentinels were sound asleep,
    But when they oped their eyes
They saw a strange, undreamed-of-sight—
    Complete was their surprise.

LIGHT HORSE HARRY AT PAULUS HOOK.

One hundred and fifty-nine that day
    Were taken prisoner,
Surprised in bed and captive led
    Ere they to arms could stir.

And on the medal that was struck
    To applaud this gallant deed
All in the Latin tongue 'tis writ,
    Which he who can may read :—

" Unhindered by opposing floods
    And bristling rampires strong,
On marched to victory and to fame
    The hero of my song.

Small was his band of followers brave,
    The greater glory theirs ;
And honor greater still than fame
    He wins from those he spares."

Such is the legend written there
    In praise of Harry Lee,
The leader of that little band
    Of dauntless cavalry.

For when the foe were in his power
    And none could lift a hand,
He spared their lives, no needless blood
    Was shed at his command.

O that such mercy as he showed
    Were known across the sea
Where ruthless Moslems wield the sword
    In fiendish cruelty.

93

LIGHT HORSE HARRY AT PAULUS HOOK.

O that we yet may see the day
When such humanity
Shall win its way in every land—
God speed that victory !

———

Inscription upon the face of the medal :—
HENRICO LEE LEGIONIS EQUIT. PRAEFECTO.
COMITIA AMERICANA.

On the obverse :—
NON OBSTANTIB. FLUMINIBUS VALLISQ.
ASTUTIA & VIRTUTE BELLICA
PARVA MANU HOSTES VICIT
VICTOSQ. ARMIS HUMANITATE DEVINXIT.
IN MEM. PUGN. AD PAULUS HOOK
DIE XIX. AUG. 1779.

Captain VOORHEES,
New Brunswick, October 26, 1779.

❈❈❈❈❈❈❈❈❈❈❈

CAPTAIN VOORHEES is off on leave
　　And glad are the thoughts that troop through his mind
As he rides all alone, for love can find
Its way to a soldier's heart and weave
On the loom of fancy a magic web
Of hopes and day-dreams and many a fair,
Bright castle upbuilt in the realms of air.
Life has its flood-tide and its ebb,
And Captain Voorhees's heart to-day
Is full of joy, near the flood of the tide,
As he rides along on his homeward way,
For to-morrow he is to claim his bride.

But who comes here ?　The militia are out !
And bring strange tidings—the mounted foe
Are raiding the land ; quick facing about,
The bridegroom must thoughts of the bride forego
And ride at the head of the men—on they pressed
In pursuit of that far-famed, dreaded band,
Simcoe's Queen's Rangers, now riding in quest
Of one whose name stands high in the land,
Governor Livingston ; with a dash
Through the Raritan Valley the Rangers ride,
Intent to leap like a lightning flash
On the rebel foe and humble his pride.

CAPTAIN VOORHEES.

Too long is the tale for me to tell;
Enough to know that, foiled of his aim,
Simcoe in the hands of the patriots fell
And failed of winning war's doubtful game.

But Captain Voorhees—what was the end
Of that day for him ?—that day when he
So joyfully on his way did wend
In hopes on the morrow a bridegroom to be.

After the fleeing foe he chased,
But just on the edge of Brunswick town
The Rangers suddenly formed and faced
And on the militia-men bore down.

Over the fence at the side of the road
The militia scramble as best they may,
For there they can fight in the primitive mode
Of Indian warfare and win the day.

But where is the Captain ?   Among the last
He plunges into the brushwood dense
Where his horse tries vainly to leap the fence
And the Rangers are charging upon him fast.

The slashing sabres rain blow on blow,
Little they reck of the morrow's bride;
Swift is the flow of his life's ebb-tide,
His life's ebb-tide with its crimson flow.

BOOK IV

1779-1780

Into WINTER CAMP on the WICKE FARM.
1779-80.

✺✺✺✺✺✺✺✺✺✺✺

'TWAS on a chill December day
    Of seventy-nine, I trow,
When a rumor came to Bottle Hill
    That filled our hearts with woe.

" Our troops have fled," so it was said,
    " And now are in retreat ;
Worse news to boot, for in pursuit
    The foe are following fleet."

That dreaded foe ! full well we know
    What horrors in the wake
Of their victorious, cruel march
    A desolation make.

No time is lost, we pack our goods,
    Prepared—'tis no disgrace—
With wives and children to retreat
    To some securer place.

But 'twas a false report, in sooth,
    The foe was not at hand ;
'Twas but the march of our patriot host
    Who fight to save our land.

Up from Short Hills they came and marched
    Through Chatham ; onward thence
In haste, until in Bottle Hill
    At dusk they pitched their tents.

Along the road they camped and when
    Next morn the sun was seen,
The smoke rose curling from their fires—
    'Tis breakfast time, I ween.

Then for the officers is spread
    The hospitable board
In houses near ; six times and more
    One house was known to afford

A morning meal to friendly guests—
    Ah ! this was better far
Than fleeing from a dreaded foe
    Beneath War's baleful star.

Anon they strike their tents and march
    To Morristown that day,
And out on the old Wicke farm they camp
    Next night, and there they stay.

Thither, to join them, comes a host
    Descending from the North
Through Pompton and Parsippany
    And Whippany, marching forth

To camp upon the old Wicke farm
    And pass the winter there ;
Ah ! bitter were the days they spent
    Where all is now so fair.

THE WINTER CAMP ON THE WICKE FARM.

A stirring sight it was to see
    Those armies marching by ;
Those from the North as they went forth
    To their encampment nigh—

One who did look hath said they took
    A day to pass the spot
Whence her young eyes beheld the sight,
    A sight she ne'er forgot.

For there were companies equipped
    With axes—pioneers—
To clear the way in time of need
    When some dense wood appears.

There were squads of horse and bands of foot,
    Rumbling artillery,
And trains of baggage-wagons—all
    Pass by promiscuously.

Across the old Morris Green they march
    And take the " mountain road"
To their winter quarters mid the hills
    And there make their abode.

With beat of drum and flying flags
    And never-ending tramp
Of horse and man they pass to reach
    That bleak mid-winter camp.

Capt. COLFAX and the LIFE GUARD.

✿✿✿✿✿✿✿✿✿✿✿✿

A ND oft a mounted troop would ride
      Along our village street ;
A noble group was that mounted troop,
      'Twas Washington and his suite.

A band of chosen men were they,
      Two hundred and two score,
Each man a born American—
      To these add ten men more.

Of character above reproach,
      Of stature good, well built ;
All in their youthful prime, I ween,
      Like knights of old, to tilt

In service of their noble chief
      And guard that manly form
On whom our weal or woe depend,
      In all this weltering storm.

Their coats were blue and faced with buff,
      And waistcoats red they wore,
With buckskin breeches, belts of white
      Around their waist ; and more,

Upon their heads cocked hats of felt,
      Black felt with white tape bound ;
In all the ranks of war's array
      No goodlier troop is found.

Well-drilled were they in every art
    Of war-like strategy,
A model for our rustic host
    In skill and loyalty.

Their Captain William Colfax was,
    A trusty warrior he,
Well pleasing to the ladies all
    For his brave gallantry.

At Bunker Hill he had fought and still
    Continued in the field
Until at Yorktown he beheld
    The British leader yield.

Thrice was he wounded—once of death
    But little did he lack,
For a bullet struck him full in front
    And came out at the back.

But in the excitement of the hour
    His hurt he did not know
And, heedless, galloped o'er the field
    Intent to check the foe.

The life-blood streamed—his men beheld
    That fatal flow and cried,
" You're hurt ! you're hurt ! fast ebbs your life !"
    Then he saw the crimson tide.

Off to the hospital he rode,
    Soon weak and faint he grew ;
But the wound was dressed ; it healed and he
    The warfare did renew.

A dashing, fiery chief was he,
    Accoutered spick and span ;
And prompt to go against the foe,
    A brave, intrepid man.

But at Pompton Plains he met his match—
    'Twas Hester Schuyler, she
Old Casper's child, a black-eyed girl
    Of roguish witchery.

True to the motto of his band,
    " I conquer or I die,"
He faced those eyes, but vainly tries
    Their victory to deny.

And when he laid the sword aside
    In seventeen eighty-three,
To Pompton Plains he came anon,
    I' faith, no time lost he.

And there fair Hester won the day,
    She conquered, yet did yield ;
And Captain Colfax led his bride
    In triumph from the field.

O well it were if on such wise
    Each deadlier strife might end ;
Love win the day, though fierce the fray,
    And each to each be friend.

Lord STIRLING'S RAID on Staten Island.
January 14, 1780.

NOW while the army was encamped
    Near Kemble Mountain there,
In January, the fourteenth day,
    Lord Stirling forth did fare

With a band of troopers bold, on sleds,
    With light artillery,
To raid the British troops upon
    The Island by the sea.

Down through New Vernon came that band
    And through Green Village soon,
And on, until through Bottle Hill,
    Late in the afternoon,

LORD STIRLING'S RAID ON STATEN ISLAND.

They passed along and in the night
    From Elizabeth Point they crossed
Upon the ice, for the Sound was bridged,
    The work of the nipping frost.

But the enemy heard of their approach
    And quickly made retreat ;
Whereat Lord Stirling's band returned,
    Their plan had met defeat.

Yet this they gained, that they returned
    With prisoners, blankets, tents,
And other spoil ; recrossed and came
    Back to their quarters whence

They had set out the day before
    To raid the red-coat foe ;
A glorious welcome is their meed
    When they their trophies show.

LORD STIRLING at the BATTLE of LONG ISLAND.

August 27, 1776.

✿✿✿✿✿✿✿✿✿✿✿✿✿

YET these are but the sports of war;
    This same Lord Stirling, he
Of Basking Ridge, it was who saw
    Our sad extremity

Upon that day in seventy-six,
    The twenty-seventh day
Of August, on Long Island, when
    He bore the palm away.

For when the Continental troops
    Were driven in defeat
Before the foe, as all men know,
    In that headlong retreat,

Lord Stirling with a little band,
    Four hundred gallant men
Of Maryland, made good his stand
    Against two thousand then.

They charged the foe, that noble band,
    Well knowing they must fall,
And yet they kept the foe at bay
    To save their comrades all.

" Good God !" cried Washington, who watched
    That all unequal fight,
" What brave men I must lose to-day !"
    And he mourned to see that sight.

Almost they drove Cornwallis back,
    But reinforcements came,
And so they lost the day, but won
    A never-dying fame.

KNYPHAUSEN'S RAID on CONNECTICUT FARMS.
June 6, 1780.

NOW on a day, 'twas the sixth of June,
    Knyphausen led the foe
In a raid wherein to Morristown
    They meant that day to go.

For much provision here was stored
    And powder and ball, they knew ;
But though they started on that raid,
    They did not quite get through.

Connecticut Farms was on their way,
    They burned it to the ground ;
And there good Parson Caldwell's wife
    With babe in arms we found

Shot down by some unfeeling wretch,
　　Who through the window fired
To slay the wife of him whose voice
　　Our patriot zeal inspired.

Maxwell of Sussex, led our men
　　And drove Knyphausen back;
While Jersey minute-men that day
　　Came swarming on his track.

KNYPHAUSEN'S RAID on SPRINGFIELD.

June 23, 1780.

AGAIN when sixteen days had passed,
　　Knyphausen led his host
Out toward Short Hills; at Springfield then
　　Our patriots, at their post,

Repelled the Red-coats by the help,
　　As you have doubtless heard,
Of Watts and Caldwell—" Give 'em Watts!"
　　Was now the inspiring word.

109

PARSON CALDWELL at Springfield, N. J.
June 23, 1780.

✿✿✿✿✿✿✿✿✿✿✿✿

SEE the Red-coats in the distance!
    Here they come! To arms! To arms!
Get your powder-horn and musket!
    Call the neighbors from their farms!

Fire the roaring eighteen-pounder
    Signal-gun from Prospect Hill!
Light the blazing black tar-barrel!
    Fight we must and fight we will!

Jump the stone wall by the road-side!
    Hide behind it! Prime your gun!
Now we're ready! See them gather!
    Farmers coming on the run!

Who's that riding in on horse-back?
    Parson Caldwell, boys; Hooray!
Red-coats call him "Fighting Chaplain;"
    How they hate him! well they may!

When he preaches to us Sundays,
    Gathered in the Old Red Store,
Down he lays his cavalry pistols,
    Sets his sentinels at the door.

Boys, remember how the British,
    Passing through Connecticut Farms,
Shot the parson's wife!—That murder
    Stirs us more than wild alarms.

Hah! The fight's begun! They're firing!
    See the flash of British steel!
Hear the crack of Jersey muskets,
    Doomed to make the Red-coats wheel!

Who's that riding on the gallop,
    Stopping by the meetin'-house door?
In he goes—comes out with arms full,
    Piled with hymn-books by the score.

Parson Caldwell!—Will he sing now,
    While the bullets round him hum?
Will he hold another meetin',
    Set the hymns to fife and drum?

Hear him shouting, " Give 'em Watts, boys!
    Put Watts into 'em, my men!"
Ah! I see, they're out of wadding;
    That's the tune! We'll all join in!

Then the worn old hymn-books fluttered,
    And their pages wildly flew,
Hither, thither, torn and dirty,
    On an errand strange and new.

Making Short Partic'lar meter,
    Parson Caldwell pitched the tunes;
Jersey farmers joined the chorus,
    Put to flight those red dragoons.

INCIDENTS OF 1779-80.

——————o————

PARSON GREEN'S CHRISTMAS TURKEY,
Hanover, 1779.

❀❀❀❀❀❀❀❀❀❀❀

NOW list to some rhymes of the olden times
    And grievous times were they,
When on every hand our goodly land
    Was smitten with dismay.

'Twas Elizabeth, the legend saith,
    The wife of Parson Green,
In Hanover village was vexed by pillage
    That deeply stirred her spleen.

" O where can be that bird ?" quoth she,
    " That turkey fine and plump ;
We've searched for him high and we've searched for him nigh,
    In tree-top and by stump.

But far and wide o'er the country-side
    Those rascally soldiers roam ;
With hungry maw they defy the law
    And eat us out of house and home."

" Now Parson Green, good Parson Green,
    I grieve to say," quoth she,
" Your Christmas dinner, thanks to some sinner,
    Is not at hand to see.

So say your grace with what grace you can,
    'Tis now the hour to dine;
May the scoundrel thief yet come to grief
    Who stole my bird so fine."

The parson, he was a godly man,
    As all good parsons be;
He loved old saws and he loved the cause
    Of glorious liberty.

Quoth he, " Good wife, thy heart is rife
    With anxious care, I know ;"
And the parson next took a Scriptural text,
    As he was wont, I trow.

" Men do not despise a thief," quoth he,
    " A hungry thief, if he steal
To satisfy the pangs that I
    Am now about to feel."

Far you may seek nor find so meek,
    So godly a man, I ween ;
Long live the fame of his honored name,
    The name of Parson Green!

A Call on LADY WASHINGTON,
January, 1780.

✿✿✿✿✿✿✿✿✿✿

"O LADY Martha Washington
  Has come to Morristown,
And we must go and quickly so,
  Each in her finest gown,
And call at Colonel Ford's to see
  That dame of high renown."

So spake the dames of Hanover
  And put on their array
Of silks to wit, and all that's fit
  To grace a gala day,
And called on lady Washington
  In raiment bright and gay.

Those were the days of scarcity
  In all our stricken land,
When hardships tried the country-side,
  Want was on every hand;
When they called on lady Washington
  In fine attire so grand.

" And don't you think! we found her with
  A speckled homespun apron on;
With knitting in hand—that lady so grand—
  That stately lady Washington!
When we came to Morristown that day
  With all our finest fixin's on!

She welcomed us right graciously
 And then, quite at her ease,
She makes the glancing needles fly
 As nimbly as you please ;
And so we found this courtly dame
 As busy as two bees."

" For while our gallant soldiers bear
 The brunt of war," quoth she,
" It is not right that we delight
 In costly finery."
So spake good Martha Washington,
 Still smiling graciously.

" But let us do our part," quoth she,
 " And speedily begin
To clothe our armies on the field
 And independence win"—
" Good-bye ! Good-bye !" we all did cry—
 " We're going home to spin!"

A FREE LUNCH at MENDHAM.
JANUARY, 1780.

✿✿✿✿✿✿✿✿✿✿

'TIS Captain David Thompson's wife,
 Of her my song shall be,
In the days of old, of hunger and cold,
 And sad extremity.

A FREE LUNCH AT MENDHAM.

One day the army marched along
    Hard by her husband's door,
In Mendham here and with good cheer
    She fed them from her store.

" No money have we to pay," said they,
    " For all your bounteous cheer;"
But still they came and blessed her name
    And all were welcome here.

" God save you, honest men," said she,
    " And may each grenadier
As quickly flee as now I see
    These good things disappear.

We'll gladly share with you whate'er
    We have, last while it may ;
Fall to with a will and eat your fill,
    We'll never rue the day."

And many such were helpful much,
    Likeminded with herself ;
The cause they served for love nor swerved
    From loyalty for pelf.

How ALEXANDER HAMILTON Gave the COUNTERSIGN.

Morristown, 1779, (about 9 P. M.)

✿✿✿✿✿✿✿✿✿✿✿

'TWAS Alexander Hamilton,
  Upon a winter's eve,
Went out to see his ladye love
  As you may well believe.

O a lady fair beyond compare,
  A ladye fair was she,
And he was a gallant officer
  Of the artillery.

An aide of Washington was he,
  We had no brighter man ;
His head was clear as a bell, they say,
  Like a flash in the powder-pan.

And yet upon this winter's eve
  It strangely did befall,
One little word, as I have heard,
  He lost beyond recall.

For in the mansion on the knoll
  Where Washington abode
He was wont to rest among the best
  Who by their chieftain rode.

And as he near the mansion came
    There met him, sooth to tell,
A sentinel true, a soldier who
    Knew Colonel Hamilton well.

" Now give the countersign," quoth he ;
    You may not cross the line,
Sure as you live, until you give
    This evening's countersign."

Then Alexander Hamilton,
    That brilliant financier,
He was non-plussed ; get past he must,
    But how, was not so clear.

For Cupid, on that winter's eve
    Had so outwitted Mars
That sentry lines and countersigns
    Were lost among the stars.

He stood amazed, he was so dazed
    He could not speak the word ;
The sentinel grim stood facing him,
    Nor from his duty stirred.

Quoth Alexander, " Let me pass ;
    You surely know me well ;
No man, I wis, shall hear of this,
    For I will never tell."

Thought the sentinel, " Surely he's trying me
    To see if I be true ;
And he shall judge, for I will not budge,
    My duty I will do."

So like a soldier true he stood
　　Nor would he weakly yield;
The Colonel may not pass, alas!
　　He's driven from the field.

Just then his eye chanced to espy,
　　Amid the gloom of night,
Young Gabriel Ford—the sight restored
　　His hopes in this sad plight.

To him he quickly called that lad
　　And whispered in his ear,
" O let me know the word, that so
　　I need no longer linger here."

That roguish lad, he was right glad
　　To please the Colonel, who
Had let him stay in the village that day
　　And had given the word that would let him through.

So in reply, as one may sigh,
　　He breathed to him the countersign,
And then with joy, thanks to the boy,
　　Great Alexander crossed the line.

How to CATCH a THIEF.

OF REVOLUTIONARY days
 A story I have heard,
That tells how once a thief was caught
 By conjuring with a bird.

A squad of soldiers made their stay
 In Belleville in those times,
And much annoyed were they by theft,
 The subject of these rhymes.

For every week when they hung out
 Their scanty clothes to dry,
They found that some were gone—forthwith
 To catch the thief they try.

One of their number they suspect
 To be that guilty thief ;
The plan they hit upon was this—
 It well might pass belief.

They took a rooster and besmeared
 This lusty chanticleer
With lamp-black o'er, then put the bird
 In a cellar dark and drear.

Each soldier next received command
 To advance and in the dark
Put forth his hand and touch this fowl,
 And when 'tis done, then hark !

120

For word is passed around that when
   The guilty man shall lay
His hand upon Sir Chanticleer
   All will be clear as day.

For the knowing fowl will loudly crow—
   A-cock-a-doodle-doo !
" Now the thief will never touch the bird,"
   Thought they, and this proved true.

For all returned from this shrewd test
   With blackened hands, save one ;
And he, as they straightway declared,
  . The deeds of theft had done.

Thus was Sir Chanticleer, in sooth,
   A bird of augury,
As truly as in ancient times
   In Greece and Italy.

A TOAST of Gen. WASHINGTON'S
1779-80.

A BALLAD ! a ballad ! and what shall it be ?
   Of the bravest young lady in New Jersee !
Ann Halsted, her name, of Elizabeth Town,
And now let me tell how she won renown.

A TOAST OF GEN. WASHINGTON'S.

Between Staten Island and Sandy Hook
The British were lying at anchor, and took
Excursions frequently down the Bay
To plunder and forage, as I've heard say.

At Halsted's Point they would often land,
And then, alert, spy-glass in hand,
At the Halsted Farm sharp watch was kept
To see if the foeman nearer crept.

The men of the house had left the farm
One day, when Ann to her great alarm,
Saw a band of red-coats coming ashore
And making straight for her father's door.

What could she do?—quick as the thought
A suit of her father's clothes she brought,
And, dressed in these, with musket in hand,
She hastens to meet the invading band.

She hides herself in a thicket dense,
And, resting her gun on the old rail fence,
She blazes away—the marauders retreat;
Dismayed at that greeting they fly to their fleet.

And when our Washington came and heard
Of her valiant deed, this was his word:
" A toast! a toast! and what shall it be ?
The bravest young lady in New Jersee !"

PARSON CHAPMAN of ORANGE.

❁❁❁❁❁❁❁❁❁❁❁

UNDER the Orange Mountain one day
    A horseman was riding upon his way,
Taking it leisurely, having no fears—
But what is that trampling of feet he hears ?

'Tis the ominous tramp of a British troop
Who are gaining on him with oath and with whoop.
He gives rein to his horse nor will he heed
The command to stop—fast flies his steed !

On ! on he flies ! They follow fleet ;
He is well in advance ; now in Ridge Street
He pauses awhile at the top of the hill
And sees them clattering after him still.

Then wheeling about and facing that troop
He waves his hat and salutes the group—
" Hurrah ! hurrah ! hurrah !" shouts he ;
" 'Three cheers ! three cheers for liberty !"

'Twas Parson Chapman—loud rang each cheer
As that troop of British horse drew near ;
They halt—" How now !—what may this mean ?
Can it be ?—it must be that the man has seen

A Yankee band beyond that hill!"
Such thoughts their hearts with terror fill.
They turn, and the sound of their horses' feet
Grows faint and fainter as they retreat.

Then Parson Chapman rode on his way
Unvexed by the foe; and, I dare say,
For his next discourse this text took he—
" Resist the devil and he will flee."

FORT NONSENSE.
1779-1780.

DIGGING on the hill,
    Digging with a will,
        Why?
Orders have gone out,
" Build a new redoubt,
        High,
On yon snowy crown,
Rising o'er the town,
        'Gainst the sky.'"

Though winter snows are deep,
Though stinging blizzards sweep

FORT NONSENSE.

O'er the hills—though we weep,
      In dismay ;
Though hunger, like a knife,
Cuts out our very life,
Though mutiny is rife,
      We obey.

Our leader finds a way,
To keep dull care at bay—
      Hurrah !
He builds a solid earth-work,
A battlement of mirth-work,
      Ha-ha !

Hurrah ! the fort is done !
Bring up the opening gun—
      Fire !
We have a strong defence,
Though hardships gather dense,
      And dire.

Cheering on the hill,
Cheering with a will—
      Why?
We've carried orders out,
We've built a new redoubt,
      High,
On this stony crown,
Rising o'er the town,
      Towards the sky.

125

1890.

A rough, unpolished stone,
Now shows where Washington,
A bloodless battle won—
          Grim the foe ;
No fires of war here flamed
To make this old fort famed—
" Fort Nonsense" it was named,
          Years ago.

Shrine of a lowly grace,
That did fierce foemen face,
          Nor fly ;
Raised on a noble base,
It lifts its rugged face,
          On high ;
For nonsense has a place,
As near as many a grace,
          To the sky.

WASHINGTON at MORRISTOWN.

WHO doth not love that great, true-hearted man
Who sojourned here a century ago
When tracks of bleeding patriots marked the snow?
Again and yet again we turn to scan
The page that shows his spirit in the van
Of hero-souls—that doth his patience show ;
Not weak, despairing patience his, I trow,
But the unswerving faith that still outran
The fleetest messengers of gaunt despair—
Hunger and cold and treachery and all
That balks a noble spirit of its aim :
His was a will upborne on wings of prayer,
A strength to endure the worst that may befall—
Though baffled, still unconquerably the same.

WASHINGTON'S HEADQUARTERS AT MORRISTOWN, N. J.

From Harper's Magazine, February, 1859.

TEMPE WICKE'S RIDE.

December 1780.

✦✦✦✦✦✦✦✦✦✦✦✦

"SORRY to trouble you, Miss; be quick,
    Get down off that horse !"—such was the word
That greeted the ears of Tempe Wicke
As she was riding home.   She demurred.

" Why should I part with my own good steed ?
What do you want of him ?"
                         Then replied
The gruff-voiced soldier, " Miss, we need
Every horse we can get, some to ride
And some for our teams, we're going away.
We've stayed here on these hills until
We can't stand it.   We want our pay.
Here we've been starving and freezing—still
We held out as well as the rest ;
But now they say that a bounty's paid
To new recruits.   It may seem best
To Congress, 'tisn't the way we're made !
We've served our time for three years past
And here we are, worse off than when
We 'listed.   Will Congress pay us last,
Us vets, after paying new men !   Why then,
We're off.   We'll start for Trenton and see

129

TEMPE WICKE'S RIDE.

What we can do.   So, Miss, get down ;
We want your horse."
                              Then temperately
Made answer Temperance Wicke to the clown
Who held her bridle—
                              " I think that stump
Would be a good place to dismount—over there !
Take care of my pet ; feed him well"—
                              with a jump
She is off—not off the horse, but the pair
Are flying at breakneck speed up the hill ;
For the soldier, taken quite off his guard,
Had loosed his hold—with watchful skill
She turned her steed, plied the whip, now hard
Up the hill they dash.   The soldiers fire
At the flying form ; but more to affright
Than harm the girl, whose worthy sire
Had sheltered their sick ; nay more, 'tis quite
A possible thing that she had nursed
Some man in that group, when taken in
At the farmer's house ; but now they cursed
And rushed up the hill with clattering din.

But she has gone and no horse is seen ;
They search the barn and the woods near by ;
Could they but peep through that shutter green
At the end of the house, they might espy
The missing steed ; for by Tempe's bed
Stands the horse, brought in at the kitchen door ;
Through the parlor next he was quickly led
And housed as he never was housed before.
There he was safely hid for a week.

The Wicke House.

From a pen and ink sketch by Miss M. Van Pelt, after the picture in
Harper's Magazine, February, 1859.

TEMPE WICKE'S RIDE.

Some officers boarded there ; they knew
And no man dared come nearer to seek
For the horse.   Erelong a mutinous crew,
A thousand strong, passed on their way
On New Year's night by the Trenton road,
To see if they could obtain their pay.

There stands the farmer's humble abode ;
Fine old mansion it was in its day,
With lion-head knocker, and near the door,
In the grass, is a stump, fast falling away,
Where stood for a hundred years and more
A great black locust—a grand old tree !
By the side of the house, like a sentinel stands
A straight red cedar, that well may be
A century old ; it still commands
A view of this pleasant country-side ;
Stands guard o'er the house where Tempe Wicke
Came home that day from a neighborly ride
At breakneck speed ; but none too quick.

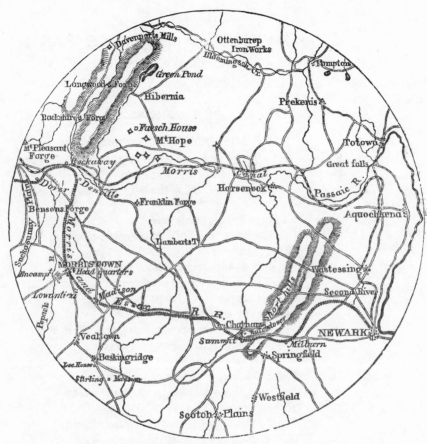

MAP OF THE VICINITY OF MORRISTOWN, NEW JERSEY.
From a MS. map by R. ERSKINE, F.R.S., used by the army, 1778-80.
Names in Italics are not in the original.

Harper's Magazine, February, 1859.

The MUTINY on the WICKE FARM near
Morristown.
January 1, 1781.

✖✖✖✖✖✖✖✖✖✖✖✖✖

THE MUTINY? Tell you more about
    Those men encamped on the old Wicke farm
Who suddenly rose and started out
    For Trenton, filling the land with alarm ?

It was the Pennsylvania line,
    The same who built, two weeks before
That breastwork of stone, the only sign,
    Almost, that remains from the days of yore
To tell of their presence on these hills—
    I mean the fort ; come, go with me ;
An old-time relic often fills
    The heart with stirring thoughts. Here see
The fort, these rude, loose piles of stone
    That stand here yet at the head of the steep
Where the leafy branches of trees, upgrown
    Since those old days, impede the sweep
Of the eye o'er landscapes fair to see—
    To Schooley's Mountain westward, and
To the south lies Basking Ridge where Lee
    Was caught like a mouse in a trap ; there stand,
On the east, Short Hills, where sentinels stood
    And beacons blazed ; around us lie

134

Or blue-tinged mountains or stream or wood,
　　Fair scenes that charm the beholder's eye.
And now we descend the hill and here
　　Is the place where lay, above Primrose brook,
The Connecticut camp, with the old road near.
　　That pile of stones was an oven to cook
Their bread ; now on by the old Fort road
　　Till we cross the brook ; here we shall find
The place where General Wayne abode
　　Near the cross-roads.　Now, if you are inclined
For a tedious tale, I will take in hand
　　To tell of the famous mutiny
That happened here in Wayne's command
　　One New Year's night, as all agree.

———

There's a hop to-night, but General Wayne
　　Has declined ; it seems all is not right
At the camp on the hill ; an army's bane,
　　The spirit of mutiny, casts its blight
Over patriot hearts ; for two weeks past
　　He has kept the men at work on a fort
That crowns the brow of yon hill, but at last
　　The old year ends and now, in short,
Their term of service is over, and they
　　With muttered threats have given it out
That they will serve no longer ; their pay
　　Is overdue ; you see, no doubt,
Why the General is not in the mood
　　To dance.　At his quarters under the hill
He stays at his post in the solitude
　　Of the evening hour, foreboding ill.

135

A clatter of hoofs on the road ! a shout !
　　Bring General Wayne to his feet, in a flash
He mounts his steed, for the troops are out !
　　And now Mad Anthony makes a dash
To turn them back.　A dauntless chief
　　Is he, far-famed for his victory
At Stony Point, where beyond belief,
　　By a bayonet charge, all silently,
He captured the fort nor fired a shot.
　　And now he confronts the mutineers ;
Cries " Halt !" but the soldiers have forgot
　　Mad Anthony's voice.　As the column nears
He aims at the leader.　In a trice
　　With twenty bayonets at his breast
The general hears this grim advice :—
　　" If you shoot," cried they, while their bayonets
　　　　pressed
Close to his heart, " 'twill be your last.
　　We love you, General ; but, don't try
To stop us now ; the time is past
　　When we obey ; if you shoot, you die."

What could he do, as face to face
　　He met that army ?　He knew they had killed
One man already ; for in the place
　　Where he faced their line, his blood was spilled ;
And there they buried him by a tree
　　On the Jockey Hollow Road, by an oak ;
Brave Captain Bettin it was, you may see
　　The place where that mutinous storm first broke.
For once brave Anthony Wayne gave in
　　And the mob marched on upon its way.

To save his life he thought no sin
    And he followed the mutineers that day
To keep them from violence in that hour
    Of lawless might ; for well he knew
The danger to all in the path of their power ;
    And " This," thought he, " is the thing to do :—
I will send supplies of food, that so
    They may not ravage the country-side,
And where they march I too will go
    And give good counsel, whate'er betide."
For General Wayne was as shrewd as brave ;
    He could madly charge in the hour of need,
But now he sought how he best might save
    The farmers from harm and turn this steed,
This runaway steed, an army astray.
    And first he advised them to take the turn
Towards Basking Ridge ; for some that day
    Appeared to make it their chief concern
To guide the army along the road
    That leads to New York, where the British that day
Were watching events ; Sir Henry forebodes
    No good to our cause. " Will these men betray
Their land for gold ?"—but the men march on.
    The alarm is given, a courier sent
To bear the tidings to Washington
    And Congress is warned, while Wayne, intent
On doing his part, attends the line
    Of insurgent troops. They still refuse
To heed his commands, though their hearts incline
    To their old-time leader, under whose
Command they had often faced the foe.

When Lafayette and St. Clair are sent
By Washington, they are given to know
    That their errand is vain ; and so matters went
For a week, while at Princeton their camp was made.
    Then President Reed to Trenton came
And had this message to Wayne conveyed
    " I will meet you, but I beg you will name
Some place outside of Princeton where
    I shall not meet with indignity
Like that late put upon St. Clair
    And Lafayette discourteously."

Then to the assembled mutineers
    Wayne read that word from the president
Of their native state, while bitter tears
    Rolled down the cheeks of the regiment.
Those bronzed and haggard faces showed
    That tender hearts lay deep within,
And felt the rebuke so justly owed
    To their breach of army discipline.

Just then in the camp two men are found
    Who offer bounties, pensions, and pay
To all who will march to the stirring sound
    Of the British drum, henceforth obey
His majesty, King George the Third.

    Then terrible wrath possessed their hearts ;
Their grievance was real, but when they heard
    Of the bribe for treason and such mean arts
They were cut to the soul.   Not a mutineer
    But made reply, " No Arnolds are we !

We've served our time, but we still can cheer
    For the glorious cause of Liberty!"
And seizing the tempters they brought them out
    To General Wayne to be tried as spies,
Thus making it plan beyond a doubt
    That they are not looking with longing eyes
To the British camp as their rendezvous;
    Though maddened by dire necessity
They still to the good old cause are true
    And gold cannot win them to treachery.

The MUTINY at POMPTON,
January 20, 1781.

WHEN word was brought to Washington
    How that the mutineers
Had compassed all they sought and gone
    Rejoicing home, grave fears
Within his breast were wakened lest
    Their case should kindle hope
In other hearts to try such arts,
    And he lays his plans to cope
With mutineers, if e'er he hears
    That ominous word again;
So he keeps at hand a trusty band
    Of full a thousand men,

Whose hearts he knew were staunch and true
    And ready at command
To uphold the right, cost what it might,
    And save our goodly land.
And this was well, for it were the knell
    Of Liberty's fair cause,
Should mutiny grow rife and be
    Unchecked by martial laws.

And now, erelong, bad tidings came
    Of trouble in the camp
At Pompton, in the Jersey line,
    And thither promptly tramp
Five hundred men of those at hand
    For such emergency,
Sent by our chief to bring relief
    And quell that mutiny.
Upon their way they quickly go
    And, marching through the night,
At break of day the mutinous camp
    Looms forth upon their sight.
Then General Robert Howe, who led
    That trusty band and true,
Marched on the tents where the sleepers lay
    And without more ado
Gave orders sharp and clear that roused
    Those slumbering mutineers;
" Fall into line without your arms !"
    They scarce believed their ears.
" Five minutes is the time I grant
    To fall in line," cried he ;
And they obeyed, too much dismayed
    To think of mutiny.

140

No time to parley then had they,
    No time to form a plan;
But into line they quickly fell,
    Obedient, to a man.
Ringleaders three were brought to trial
    And one a pardon found;
But two were shot upon the spot
    And buried in the ground.
Such was the end of the darkest hour
    That came before the day,
For victory crowned our cause erelong,
    And Yorktown changed our griefs to song
And drove our fears away.

Victory at Yorktown, October 19, 1781.

CHATHAM BRIDGE.

NOT far to seek is Chatham Bridge
    As on the highway you may ride
From Morristown along the ridge
    To Madison; here let us bide
A moment—list! the ghostly tramp
Of troops who once came here to camp.

Then on we ride through Chatham, till
    The Chatham Bridge at last we reach;

Here as we rest let memory fill
    The mind with what this spot can teach ;
Here let us think of the days of old
And tales that of those times are told.

Hither came all who sought to cross
    Passaic's stream and onward fare ;
Here guards were set, for it were loss
    If o'er this bridge the foe should dare
To pass and raid the land or make
Some prisoner—all was here at stake.

A company was ordered here
    By good Benoni Hathaway
Of Morristown ; it doth appear
    In pension lists of that far day,
That they were led, that company,
By Timothy Tuttle of Whippany.

And here on guard stood Ashbel Green
    A little time as sentinel,
When but a youth; his age, I ween,
    Was fifteen years, yet he guarded well
This Chatham Bridge and made arrest
Of one whose case was none the best.

And here it was that General Winds
    Met a British officer afield ;
Here those two warriors spoke their minds
    And the Briton thought it best to yield ;
So Winds escorted him on his way
As he retreated home that day.

These are but trifling tales, in sooth,
    And yet they point to matters fraught
With destiny, this is but truth,
    As you shall quickly now be taught;
'Tis in the annals of our State
With other matters small and great.

1779-80.

On Kemble Hill our army lay
    And Washington his quarters had
In Morristown amd made his stay
    At Colonel Ford's, as I may add;
When forth there rode a daring force,
A squadron of the British horse.

From Staten Island on they came
    And in the night they took their way;
They passed the sentinels, the same
    That at Short Hills were set to stay
Marauding bands; o'er Chatham Bridge
They crossed, and started up the ridge

To Bottle Hill; but snow and hail
    Had clogged their speed through all the night;
They saw their plan would surely fail
    And back they turned in sorry plight;
For their steeds were lamed by the icy crust
That cut their feet—retreat they must.

143

CHATHAM BRIDGE.

Their guide, he was I know not who,
    But that he was an American ;
And, fearing he would not be true
    Unto their cause, they set the man
Within a hollow square, and so,
Swords drawn, in haste they homeward go.

Back to the Point they safely rode
    To which they had crossed when they set out
From Staten Island, their abode.
    'Twas known then what they were about,
And moved was all the country-side
On hearing of that midnight ride.

For had their errand met success,
    What it had wrought, no man can say ;
Our cause had been one man the less ;
    One man the less, mean what that may ;
Ah ! had they stolen our Washington,
Our cause, God wot, had been undone !

BOOK V

1780-1781

The WASHINGTON HEADQUARTERS,

MORRISTOWN.

✿✿✿✿✿✿✿✿✿✿✿✿

WHAT mean these cannon standing here,
These staring, muzzled dogs of war?
Heedless and mute, they cause no fear,
Like lions caged, forbid to roar.

This gun was made when good Queen Anne
Ruled upon Merry England's throne ;
Captured by valiant Jerseymen
Ere George the Third our rights would own.

" Old Nat," the little cur on wheels,
Protector of our sister city,
Was kept to bite the British heels,
A yelping terror, bold and gritty.

---

1. Inscription on this cannon:—
    This gun was made in Queen Anne's time. Captured with a British vessel
        by a party of Jerseymen in the year 1780, near Perth Amboy.
    Presented by the township of Woodbridge. New Jersey, 1874.

2. Inscription on '' Old Nat:''—
    This cannon was furnished Capt. Nathaniel Camp by Gen. George Wash-
        ington for the protection of Newark, N. J., against the British.
    Presented to the Association by Mr. Bruen H. Camp of Newark, N. J.

That savage beast, the " Old Crown Prince,"
    A British bull-dog, glum, thick-set,
At Springfield's fight was made to wince
    And now we keep him for a pet.

Upon this grassy knoll they stand,
    A venerable, peaceful pack ;
Their throats once tuned to music grand,
    And stained with gore their muzzles black.

But come, that portal swinging free
    A welcome offers as of yore,
When, sheltered 'neath this old roof-tree,
    Our patriot chieftain trod this floor.

And with him in that trying day
    Was gathered here a glorious band ;
This house received more chiefs, they say,
    Than any other in our land.

Hither magnanimous Schuyler came,
    And stern Steuben from o'er the water ;
Here Hamilton, of brilliant fame, once met and courted
    Schuyler's daughter.

---

3.   The " Crown Prince" is the largest of the three cannon that now stand at
the western end of the building. It was captured from the British at
Springfield, N. J.

4.   The list of officers of the Revolutionary army mentioned in the poem is
taken from a printed placard which hangs in the hall of Headquarters.

And Knox, who leads the gunner-tribes,
    Whose shot the trembling foeman riddles,—
A roaring chief, his cash subscribes
    To pay the mirth-inspiring fiddles.

The fighting Quaker, General Greene,
    Helped Knox to foot the fiddler's bill ;
And here the intrepid " Put" was seen,
    And Arnold,—black his memory still.

And Kosciusko, scorning fear ;
    Beside him noble Lafayette ;
And gallant " light-horse Harry" here
    His kindly chief for counsel met.

" Mad Anthony" was here a guest ;
    Madly he charged, but shrewdly planned ;
And many another in whose breast
    Was faithful counsel for our land.

Among those worthies was a dame
    Of mingled dignity and grace ;
Linked with the warrior-statesman's fame
    Is Martha's comely, smiling face.

---

5.   The reference to the fiddlers is based upon an old subscription paper for defraying the expenses of a " Dancing Assembly," signed by several persons, among them Nathaniel Greene and H. Knox, each $400, *paid*. This sum was about equivalent to ten dollars in cash, as the paper money of the day was greatly depreciated.

6.   Knox is called a roaring chief because, when crossing the Delaware with Washington, his "stentorian lungs" did good service in keeping the army together.

CHAIR AND DESK USED BY WASHINGTON
AT MORRISTOWN. N. J.
From Harper's Magazine, February, 1859.

Bnt look around, to right, to left;
    Pass through these rooms, once Martha's pride;
The dining-hall of guests bereft,
    The kitchen with its fire-place wide.

See the huge logs, the swinging crane,
    The Old Man's Seat by chimney ingle;
The pots and kettles, all the train
    Of brass and pewter, here they mingle.

In the large hall above, behold
    The flags, the eagle poised for flight;
While sabres, bayonets, flint-locks old
    Tell of the struggle and the fight.

Old faded letters bear the seal
    Of men who battled for a stamp;
A cradle and a spinning-wheel
    Bespeak the home behind the camp.

Apartments opening from the hall
    Show chairs and desks of quaint old style;
And curious pictures on the wall
    Provoke a reverential smile.

Musing, we loiter in each room
    And linger with our vanished sires;
We hear the deep, far-echoing boom
    That spoke of old in flashing fires.

But deepening shadows bid us go,
    The western sun is sinking fast;
We take our leave with foot-steps slow,—
    Farewell, ye treasures of the past!

THE WASHINGTON HEADQUARTERS AT MORRISTOWN.

A century has come and gone
    Since these old relics saw their day ;
That day was but the opening dawn
    Of one that has not passed away.

Our banner is no worthless rag,
    With patriot pride hearts still beat high ;
And there, above, still waves the flag
    For which our fathers dared to die.

THE WASHINGTON HEADQUARTERS,
MORRISTOWN, NEW JERSEY.

From a Photograph by James Madison Todd, February 25, 1896.

In a WHEAT FIELD.

Near Morristown, on the old Wicke Farm, where the American army had a hospital and a burial ground in the Revolutionary War. The stone chimneys of several of the huts referred to may still be seen in the woods on the hill over-looking Leddell's pond.

———

A CORN of wheat abides alone
     Except it fall to earth and die ;
   There if it for a season lie
Concealed from view, perchance unknown,

Should heaven vouchsafe its gracious smile
     And shed its dews upon that grave
     A golden harvest soon shall wave
And reapers garner it erewhile.

In its dark tomb the buried grain
     Has linked its life with Nature's might,
     Has triumphed o'er the powers of night
And turned our seeming loss to gain.

We talk of wheat—we lift our eyes
     And see the field where late it stood;
     A rising slope to yonder wood
From the green copse that lower lies.

And in the midst a locust grove
  With tall, slim trunks that seek the sky ;
  Their shade invites the passer-by
To stay the steps that hither rove.

The locusts bow their leafy heads
  And murmur to the wandering breeze,
  And 'neath the shadow of the trees
Sleep warriors in their peaceful beds.

No world-famed victory marked this place,
  No man can name the silent dead,
  Yet men draw near with reverent tread
And talk with spirits, face to face.

'Twas on this field they camped of old,
  Beside yon stream, and battled long
  With hunger, sickness, want—a throng
Of foes grown fierce in winter's cold.

Scarce sheltered from the biting frost
  Beneath rude huts, they fed the fires
  Of Freedom with their funeral pyres
To save the spark that else were lost.

They yielded not to mortal foe
  Nor fled dishonored from the field,
  But Death's stern summons bade them yield
And lay their heads beneath the snow.

A corn of wheat, except it die
  Abides alone ; but lost in earth,
  Reveals at last its hidden worth—
We reap the fields where heroes lie.

154

ENGLAND and AMERICA.

1896.

TO any student of history it is clear that the American Rev-
lution was not a conflict between Americans and English-
men so much as it was a continuation of the struggle which
Englishmen had themselves carried on for centuries in their
own land against the tyranny of unjust rulers.

Magna Carta was one step towards the American Declar-
ation of Independence. The Revolution of Oliver Cromwell
and John Milton, by the united forces of sword and pen, was
another. Out of that national upheaval in old England came
the spirit of New England. The Declaration of Independence
in the new England that had grown up in America was but the
capstone of the history that had been making in the mother
country ever since Caesar invaded Britain.

VICTORIA, queen of that fair isle
In which the cause of Freedom rose,
Century by century, mid fierce throes
That rent thine ancient realm the while,
On us bestow thy kindliest smile ;
Reck not of those hard-handed blows
In anguish struck ; no more as foes
Armed to the teeth and shod with guile

Regard us ; but recall the ties,
Endearing ties, that still unite
Great ALBION to her offspring ; pray
In all sincerity that wise,
New-era-ushering men may plight
A vow of peace to last for aye.

August 5, 1896.

Extract from the Annual Address before the American Bar Association by the Right Honorable Lord Russell of Killowen; LL. D., G. C. M. G., etc., Lord Chief Justice of England. Delivered at Saratoga, N. Y., August 20, 1896 :—

TRUE CIVILIZATION.

In dealing with the subject of arbitration I have thought it right to sound a note of caution, but it would, indeed, be a reproach to our nineteen centuries of Christian civilization if there were now no better method for settling international differences than the cruel and debasing methods of war. May we not hope that the people of these States and the people of the mother land—kindred peoples—may, in this matter, set an example of lasting influence to the world? They are blood relations. They are indeed separate and independent peoples, but neither regards the other as a foreign nation.

We boast of our advance and often look back with pitying contempt on the ways and manners of generations gone by. Are we ourselves without reproach? Has our civilization borne the true marks? Must it not be said, as has been said of religion itself, that countless crimes have been committed in its name? Probably it was inevitable that the weaker races should in the end succumb; but have we always treated them with consideration and with justice? Has not civilization too often been presented to them at the point of the bayonet and the Bible by the hand of the fillibuster? And apart from races we deem barbarous, is not the passion for dominion and wealth and power accountable for the worst chapters of cruelty and oppression written in the world's history? Few people—perhaps none—are free from this reproach. What, indeed, is true civilization? By its fruit you shall know it. It is not dominion, weath, material luxury; nay, not even a great literature and education widespread—good though these things be. Civilization is not a veneer; it must penetrate to the very heart and core of societies of men.

Its true signs are thought for the poor and suffering, chivalrous regard and respect for woman, the frank recognition of human brotherhood irrespective of race or color or nation or religion, the narrowing of the domain of mere force as a governing factor in the world, the love of ordered freedom, abhorrence of what is mean and cruel and vile, ceaseless devotion to the claims of justice. Civilization in that, its true, its highest sense, must make for peace. We have solid grounds for faith in the future. Government is becoming more and more, but in no narrow class sense, government of the people, by the people and for the people. Populations are no longer moved and manoeuvred as the arbitrary will or restless ambition or caprice of kings or potentates may dictate. And although democracy is subject to violent gusts of passion and prejudice, they are gusts only. The abiding sentiment of the masses is for peace—for peace to live industrious lives and to be at rest with all mankind. With the prophet of old they feel—though the feeling may find no articulate utterance—" how beautiful upon the mountains are the feet of him that bringeth good tidings, that publisheth peace."

Mr. President, I began by speaking of the two great divisions—American and British—of that English-speaking world which you and I represent to-day, and with one more reference to them I end.

Who can doubt the influence they possess for insuring the healthy progress and the peace of mankind? But if this influence is to be fully felt, they must work together in cordial friendship, each people in its own spere of action. If they have great power, they have also great responsibility. No cause they espouse can fail; no cause they oppose can triumph. The future is, in large part, theirs. They have the making of history in the times that are to come. The greatest calamity that could befall would be strife which should divide them.

Let us pray that this shall never be. Let us pray that they, always self respecting, each in honor upholding its own flag, safeguarding its own heritage of right and respecting the rights of others, each in its own way fulfilling its high national destiny, shall yet work in harmony for the progress and the peace of the world.

UNANIMOUS FOR ARBITRATION.

The report on " International Law" recommended that the American Bar Association concur in the following resolutions adopted by the American Conference on International Arbitration at Washington in April :—

First—That in the judgment of this Conference religion, humanity and justice, as well as the material interests of civilized society, demand the immediate establishment between the United States and Great Britain of a permanent system of arbitration, and the earliest possible extension of such a system to embrace all civilized nations.

Second—That it is earnestly recommended to our Government, so soon as it is assured of a corresponding disposition on the part of the British Government, to negotiate a treaty providing for the widest practical application of the method of arbitration to international controversies.

Third—That a committee of this Conference be appointed to prepare and present to the President of the United States a memorial respectfully urging the taking of such steps on the part of the United States as will best conduce to the end in view.

These resolutions were unanimously carried.

A CALENDAR of the REVOLUTION

Showing Events in New Jersey in their Relation to the War as a whole.

❀❀❀❀❀❀❀❀❀❀

PREMONITIONS.

1765.	The Stamp Act.
1768.	Boston occupied by Troops.
1770.	The Boston Massacre.
1773.	The Boston Tea Party.
1774.	First Continental Congress; Philadelphia.

THE WAR FOR INDEPENDENCE.

1775.

April 19.	Lexington and Concord.
	Siege of Boston.
June 15.	Washington appointed Commander-in-chief.
	His journey to Boston.
June 17.	Bunker Hill.

1776. WINTER CAMP AROUND BOSTON.

March 17.	Boston evacuated.
July 4.	Declaration of Independence.
August 27.	Battle of Long Island.
	Washington's retreat across New Jersey.
November 16.	Ft. Washington taken by the British.
December 13.	Gen. Lee captured at Basking Ridge.
26.	Washington's victory at Trenton.

1777.

January 3.	Princeton; Washington—Cornwallis.
6.	Washington enters Morristown.

159

1777.   WINTER CAMP IN LOANTAKA VALLEY.
April 13.   Cornwallis surprises Gen.Lincoln at Bound Brook.
May 28.   Washington marches to Middlebrook.
             Howe maneuvers in front of the camp.
June 30.   Howe withdraws from New Jersey.
             Washington chasing Howe's fleet.
July 4.   "   at Morristown one week.
    22.   "   at the Hudson.
    28.   "   at Bedminster, en route to Phila.
    30.   "   at the Delaware River.
July,   Burgoyne comes down from Canada.
August 1.   Some troops sent back towards the Hudson;
             but Washington stays in Pennsylvania.
August 16.   Bennington; Stark—Baum.
             Howe enters Chesapeake Bay;
             Gen. Lee, a prisoner, advises Howe.
September 11. Brandywine; Washington—Howe.
September 19. Bemis Heights I. ; Arnold—Burgoyne.
    26.   Cornwallis enters Philadelphia.
October 4.   Germantown; Washington—Howe.
    7.   Bemis Heights II. ; Arnold—Burgoyne.
    17.   Burgoyne surrenders to Gates at Saratoga.
             Conway Cabal; comparisons between German-
             town and Saratoga.
December 18. The army moves into camp at Valley Forge.

1778.   WINTER CAMP AT VALLEY FORGE.
             Steuben drills the army.
February 6. Franklin effects a Treaty with France.
May 11.   Death of Lord Chatham.
             Sir Wm. Howe resigns his command;
             Sir Henry Clinton succeeds him.
June 18.   British evacuate Philadelphia.
             Sir Henry Clinton's march to New York.
    28.   Monmouth; Washington—Clinton.
July 4.   Washington's army rests at New Brunswick on
             the Raritan. Trial of Gen. Lee begun.

1778.

July 4.   Massacre at Wyoming, Penn.; Butler and Brandt.
July 20.   Washington's Headquarters at White Plains, N.Y.
December 12. The army moves into camp at Middlebrook.
     29. The British take Savannah.

1779.   WINTER CAMP AT MIDDLEBROOK.
February 18. Grand Fete and Ball at Pluckamin.
            Steuben's drill-book—drills the army.
            No fighting at this camp; society.
            Hamilton and Colfax are stars.
May 2.   Grand Review at Bound Brook for the European
            Envoys.
May 14.   Grand Review for the Indian Envoys.
May to Nov. Sullivan's Expedition against the Six Nations.
June & July. Washington marched to Highlands on Hudson.
July 15.   Stony Point captured by Gen. Wayne.
    22,   Battle of Minisink : Hathorn–Brandt.
August 19.   Harry Lee surprises Paulus Hook.
September 23. Paul Jones and the Bonhomme Richard.
October 26. Simcoe's Raid through the Raritan Valley.
            Conquest of Georgia by British.
December 7. The army moves into Camp near Morristown.

1780.   WINTER CAMP on the WICKE FARM.
            Mrs. Washington arrives at Morristown.
            The Great Blizzard; suffering.
January 14. Lord Stirling's raid on Staten Island.
    26,   Arnold Sentenced.
April 19,   Grand Parade for Luzerne & Miralles, Morrist'n.
            Funeral of Don Juan de Miralles.
May 12.   British take Charleston.
   15.   Mutiny of the Connecticut line; hence
            Knyphausen's Raid on Connecticut Farms.
June 21.   Washington goes to Pompton en route for West
            Point; hence
June 23.   Knyphausen's Second Raid ; Springfield.
            Conquest of South Carolina by British.
July 10.   French Fleet at Newport, R. I.

August 16.   Camden; Gates (Southern Willows.)
September 18.   Washington crosses Hudson at West Point, goes
                to Hartford; meantime occurs
September 21.   Arnold's Treason at West Point.
                Greene takes command in the South.
December,   Washington's Headquarters at New Windsor on
                Hudson, from December 1780 till June 1781.
                WINTER CAMPS:—PENN. line at Morristown,
                                N. J. "   " Pompton,
                                N. E. "   " West Point,
                                N. Y. "   " Albany.

1781.   Wayne's WINTER CAMP NEAR MORRISTOWN on
                the Wicke Farm.
January 1.   Mutiny of Penn. troops near Morristown.
January 17.   Cowpens; Morgan–Tarleton.
      20.   Mutiny of New Jersey troops at Pompton.
March 15.   Guilford Court House; Greene–Cornwallis.
August,   Washington encamps at Morristown (a Ruse).
                on his way to Yorktown.
September 8.   Eutaw Springs; Greene–Stuart.
October 19,   Yorktown.   Cornwallis surrenders.
                SUSPENSION OF HOSTILITIES.

1782.
April 19.   News received that the Independence of the
                United States is acknowledged.
April,   Washington's Headquarters at Newburgh, two
                miles above New Windsor, most of the time
                until November 1783.
1783.
September 3.   PEACE CONCLUDED.
November 25.   New York Evacuated by the British.
December,   The Army Disbands.
December 23.   Washington lays down his commission in New
                York City.

NOTES.

A Tory.—The tory element has not been made as prominent in these ballads as it really was.

Esek Ryno lived at Dog Corners, about two and a half miles from Plainfield on the Plainfield, and Raritan road, opposite the old Dog Tavern. This region is called Short Hills; but the "Lookout at Short Hills" was just above Springfield.

Washington at Brandywine.—This incident was related to me by a friend, who said that it was given in some historical work by an English author.

An Incident at the Battle of Monmouth.—Dr. Joseph F. Tuttle states that this incident was related to him by Dr. Charles G. McChesney, whose grandmother is the one referred to in the ballad.

In connection with the Battle of Monmouth I add a short piece, written for one of my younger pupils to speak. It proved to be well adapted to its purpose and was quite popular.

A holiday in BOTTLE HILL.

About June 30, 1778.

❊❊❊❊❊❊❊❊❊❊

SAY JABEZ, where are you going?
    You're walking in your sleep!
No school to-day! hooray! hooray!
    This news is too good to keep!

What for? I'll tell you, Jabez;
    You see, our army won
The fight last Sunday at Monmouth
    And now we'll see some fun.

They're going to celebrate the day
    Up here in Bottle Hill;
So the teacher gave us a holiday
    And celebrate we will.

I'm going to get my cannon
    And ram the powder down,
And when she bangs, look out, old boy!
    They'll hear it all over town.

And Josiah Burnet's coming
    To celebrate with me;
We'll show 'em how to celebrate,
    You just come up and see !

These verses are based upon the fact, recorded in the Tuttle papers, that Rev. Ebenezer Bradford of Bottle Hill, gave his schoolboys a holiday when the news of the battle was received. His school was situated where the R. R. station now is.

GEN. KNOX.—Dr. Honeyman, in commenting on the action of this Dutch church, says that it was not in accord with the usual liberality of the Dutch in that day.

AN EARNEST OF VICTORY.—This story is very happily told by John Fiske in his American Revolution, vol. II, 51; but history does not record that Captain Fairlie sang this song on the occasion of the Banquet at Bound Brook.

THE BATTLE OF MINISINK.—On July 22, 1822, the people of Orange County, N. Y., dedicated a monument to the memory of those who fell at the battle of Minisink (New Jersey.)

HUMANITY IN WAR.—Extract from Lord Russell's address before the Bar Association, Saratoga, August 20, 1896:- A bare recital of some of the important respects in which the evils of war have been mitigated by more humane customs must suffice.

NOTES.

Among them are : 1. The greater immunity from attack of the persons and property of enemy-subjects in a hostile country. 2. The restrictions imposed on the active operations of a belligerent when occupying an enemy's country. 3. The recognized distinction between subjects of the enemy, combatant and non-combatant. 4. The deference accorded in cartels, safe-conducts and flags of truce. 5. The protection secured for ambulances and hospitals, and for all engaged in tending the sick and wounded—of which the Geneva Red Cross Convention of 1864 is a notable illustration. 6. The condemnation of the use of instruments of warfare which cause needless suffering.

In this field of humane work the United States took a prominent part. When the Civil War broke out, President Lincoln was prompt in intrusting to Professor Franz Lieber the duty of preparing a manual of systematized rules for the conduct of forces in the field—rules aimed at the prevention of those scenes of cruelty and rapine which were formerly a disgrace to humanity. That manual has, I believe, been utilized by the Governments of England, France and Germany.

Even more important are the charges wrought in the position of neutrals in war times, who, while bound by strict obligations, of neutrality, are in great measure left free and unrestricted in the pursuit of peaceful trade.

PARSON CALDWELL AT SPRINGFIELD.—Bret Harte's spirited poem on this subject is well known.

HOW ALEXANDER HAMILTON GAVE THE COUNTERSIGN.— The lady referred to was Elizabeth Schuyler, the daughter of Gen. Philip Schuyler, whose headquarters were not far off.

TEMPE WICKE'S RIDE.—This story was related to me by Miss Elizabeth Leddell, a descendant of Tempe Wicke's sister. I have followed her version of the story, which differs in some significant details from any printed version that I have seen.

IN A WHEAT FIELD.—I visited this place, in July 1893, when the wheat surrounding the locust grove had just been harvested.

A NUMBER of these ballads, selected to illustrate MORRIS COUNTY IN THE REVOLUTION, were spoken by the pupils of MORRIS ACADEMY at a public entertainment, in June, 1896.

INDEX.

166

INDEX.

ERRATUM.

Page 22. In the line "Ere you will find him here," the word "here" is a misprint for "there."